DATE DUE

GAYLORD			PRINTED IN U.S.A.

MAN IS NOT ALONE

●

MAN IS NOT ALONE

A Philosophy of Religion

ABRAHAM JOSHUA HESCHEL

Farrar, Straus and Giroux / New York

Farrar, Straus and Giroux
19 Union Square West, New York 10003

Copyright © 1951 by Abraham Joshua Heschel,
renewed 1979 by Sylvia Heschel
All rights reserved
Distributed in Canada by Douglas & McIntyre Ltd.
Printed in the United States of America
Published in 1951 by Farrar, Straus and Giroux
First paperback edition, 1976

Paperback ISBN: 0-374-51328-7

EAN: 978-0-374-51328-3

Designed by Marshall Lee

www.fsgbooks.com

31   33   35   36   34   32   30

CONTENTS

BEYOND THINGS
A SPIRITUAL PRESENCE

FROM HIS PRESENCE TO HIS ESSENCE
THE DAWN OF FAITH
WHAT TO DO WITH WONDER
WHO IS THE ENIGMA?
THE INVINCIBLE QUESTION
IN SEARCH OF A SOUL
THE PREMISE OF PRAISE
LET THE INSIGHT BE
GOD IS SUING FOR MAN
THE ENFORCED CONCERN

FAITH IS NO SHORT CUT
WAYS TO FAITH
SOME OF US BLUSH
THE TEST OF FAITH
AN ACT OF SPIRIT

THE PERIL OF SPEECH
STANDARDS OF EXPRESSION
WHAT DO WE MEAN BY THE DIVINE?
THE ATTRIBUTE OF PERFECTION
THE IDEA OF THE UNIVERSE
COSMIC BROTHERHOOD

COMPASSION
DISPLAY AND DISGUISE

THE PERIL OF FAITH
TO BELIEVE IS TO REMEMBER
FAITH AS INDIVIDUAL MEMORY
FAITH AND BELIEF
FAITH AND CREED
THE IDOLATRY OF DOGMAS
ARE DOGMAS NECESSARY?
FAITH AND REASON
"GRANT US KNOWLEDGE . . ."
FAITH IS RECIPROCITY
RELIGION IS MORE THAN INWARDNESS

II. The problem of living

FROM WONDER TO PIETY
THE PROBLEM OF THE NEUTRAL
THE EXPERIENCE OF NEEDS
LIFE—A CLUSTER OF NEEDS
THE INADEQUACY OF ETHICS
THE PERIL OF LIVING
NEEDS ARE NOT HOLY
WHO KNOWS HIS REAL NEEDS?
RIGHT AND WRONG NEEDS

I. THE PROBLEM OF GOD

1 The Sense of the Ineffable

There are three aspects of nature which command man's attention: power, loveliness, grandeur. Power he exploits, loveliness he enjoys, grandeur fills him with awe. We take it for granted that man's mind should be sensitive to nature's loveliness. We take it equally for granted that a person who is not affected by the vision of earth and sky, who has no eyes to see the grandeur of nature and to sense the sublime, however vaguely, is not human.

But why? What does it do for us? The awareness of grandeur does not serve any social or biological purpose; man is very rarely able to portray his appreciation of the sublime to others or to add it to his scientific knowledge. Nor is its perception pleasing to the senses or gratifying to our vanity. Why, then, expose ourselves to the disquieting provocation of something that defies our drive to know, to something which may even fill us with fright, melancholy or resignation? Still we insist that it is unworthy of man not to take notice of the sublime.

Perhaps more significant than the fact of our awareness of

3

the cosmic is our consciousness of *having to* be aware of it, as if there were an *imperative*, a compulsion to pay attention to that which lies beyond our grasp.

The power of expression is not the monopoly of man. Expression and communication are, to some degree, something of which animals are capable. What characterizes man is not only his ability to develop words and symbols, but also his being compelled to draw a distinction between the utterable and the unutterable, to be stunned by that which is but cannot be put into words.

It is the sense of the sublime that we have to regard as the root of man's creative activities in art, thought and noble living. Just as no flora has ever fully displayed the hidden vitality of the earth, so has no work of art ever brought to expression the depth of the unutterable, in the sight of which the souls of saints, poets and philosophers live. The attempt to convey what we see and cannot say is the everlasting theme of mankind's unfinished symphony, a venture in which adequacy is never achieved. Only those who live on borrowed words believe in their gift of expression. A sensitive person knows that the intrinsic, the most essential, is never expressed. Most—and often the best—of what goes on in us is our own secret; we have to wrestle with it ourselves. The stirring in our hearts when watching the star-studded sky is something no language can declare. What smites us with unquenchable amazement is not that which we grasp and are able to convey but that which lies

4

within our reach but beyond our grasp; not the quantitative aspect of nature but something qualitative; not what is beyond our range in time and space but the true meaning, source and end of being, in other words, the ineffable.

THE ENCOUNTER WITH THE INEFFABLE

The ineffable inhabits the magnificent and the common, the grandiose and the tiny facts of reality alike. Some people sense this quality at distant intervals in extraordinary events; others sense it in the ordinary events, in every fold, in every nook; day after day, hour after hour. To them things are bereft of triteness; to them being does not mate with non-sense. They hear the stillness that crowds the world in spite of our noise, in spite of our greed. Slight and simple as things may be—a piece of paper, a morsel of bread, a word, a sigh—they hide and guard a never-ending secret: A glimpse of God? Kinship with the spirit of being? An eternal flash of a will?

Part company with preconceived notions, suppress your leaning to reiterate and to know in advance of your seeing, try to see the world for the first time with eyes not dimmed by memory or volition, and you will detect that you and the things that surround you—trees, birds, chairs—are like parallel lines that run close and never meet. Your pretense of being acquainted with the world is quickly abandoned.

How do we seek to apprehend the world? Intelligence inquires into the nature of reality, and, since it cannot work without its tools, takes those phenomena that appear to fit its categories as answers to its inquiry. Yet, when trying to hold an interview with reality face to face, without the aid of either words or concepts, we realize that what is intelligible to our mind is but a thin surface of the profoundly undisclosed, a ripple of inveterate silence that remains immune to curiosity and inquisitiveness like distant foliage in the dusk.

IS THERE AN ENTRANCE TO THE ESSENCE?

Analyze, weigh and measure a tree as you please, observe and describe its form and functions, its genesis and the laws to which it is subject; still an *acquaintance* with its *essence* never comes about. Looking at things through the medium of our thoughts remains an act of crystal-gazing; the pictures we induce happen to be part of the truth, nevertheless, what we see is a mental image, not the things themselves. Hastily running down the narrow path of time, man and world have no station, no present, where they can get acquainted. Thinking is never co-temporal with its object, for it follows the process of perception that took place previously. We always deal in our thoughts with posthumous objects. Acting always behind perception, thinking has only memories at its disposal. Its object is a matter of the past, like a moment before the last: so close and so far away. Knowledge, therefore, is a set of reminiscences, and, our perception being always incomplete and full of omissions, a subsequent combination of random memories. We rarely discover, we remember before we think; we see the present in the light of what we already know. We constantly compare instead of penetrate, and are never entirely unprejudiced. Memory is often a hindrance to creative experience.

6

Man is not alone

Thinking is fettered in words, in names, and names describe that which things have in common. The individual and unique in reality is not captured by names. Yet our mind necessarily compromises with words, with names. This is an additional reason why we rarely find the entrance to the essence. We cannot even adequately say what it is that we miss.

Is it necessary to ascend the pile of ideas in order to learn that our solutions are enigmas, that our words are indiscretions? A world of things is open to our minds, but often it appears as if the mind were a sieve in which we try to hold the flux of reality, and there are moments in which the mind is swept away by the tide of the unexplorable, a tide usually stemmed but never receding.

THE DISPARITY OF SOUL AND REASON

The awareness of the unknown is earlier than the awareness of the known. The tree of knowledge grows upon the soil of mystery. Next to our mind are not concepts, words, names, but the nameless, the inexpressible, being. For while it is true that the given, the apparent is next *to* our experience; *within* experience it is otherness, remoteness, upon which we come. Concepts are delicious snacks with which we try to alleviate our amazement. Try to think reality itself, forget what you know, and you realize at once your distressing famishment. We should not expect thoughts to give us more than what they contain. Soul and reason are *not* the same. It seems as if concepts and our own selves were strangers who somewhere in the endlessness of time met and became friends. They often mate and often alienate, for the benefit of both. The more incisive the awareness of the unknown and the more sustaining our immediate grasp of reality, the more trenchant and unrelenting becomes our realization of that disparity.

Just as the simple-minded equates appearance with reality, so does the overwise equate the expressible with the ineffable, the logical with the metalogical, concepts with things. And just as critical thought is conscious of its not being identical with things, so does our self-reflecting soul bear in its heart an awareness of itself, distinct from the logical content of its thoughts.

The awareness of the ineffable is that with which our search must begin. Philosophy, enticed by the promise of the known, has often surrendered the treasures of higher incomprehension to poets and mystics, although without the sense of the ineffable there are no metaphysical problems, no awareness of being as being, of value as value.

The search of reason ends at the shore of the known; on the immense expanse beyond it only the sense of the ineffable can glide. It alone knows the route to that which is remote from experience and understanding. Neither of them is amphibious: reason cannot go beyond the shore, and the sense of the ineffable is out of place where we measure, where we weigh.

We do not leave the shore of the known in search of adventure or suspense or because of the failure of reason to answer our questions. We sail because our mind is like a fantastic sea shell, and when applying our ear to its lips we hear a perpetual murmur from the waves beyond the shore.

Citizens of two realms, we all must sustain a dual allegiance: we sense the ineffable in one realm, we name and exploit reality in another. Between the two we set up a system of references, but we can never fill the gap. They are as far and as close to each other as time and calendar, as violin and melody, as life and what lies beyond the last breath.

The tangible phenomena we scrutinize with our reason, the sacred and indemonstrable we overhear with the sense of the ineffable. The force that inspires readiness for self-sacrifice, the thoughts that breed humility within and behind the mind, are not identical with the logician's craftsmanship. The purity of which we never cease to dream, the untold things we insatiably love, the vision of the good for which we either die or perish alive—no reason can bound. It is the ineffable from which we draw the taste of the sacred, the joy of the imperishable.

2 Radical Amazement

The greatest hindrance to knowledge is our adjustment to conventional notions, to mental clichés. Wonder or radical amazement, the state of maladjustment to words and notions, is, therefore, a prerequisite for an authentic awareness of that which is.

Standing eye to eye with being as being, we realize that we are able to look at the world with two faculties—with reason and with wonder. Through the first we try to explain or to adapt the world to our concepts, through the second we seek to adapt our minds to the world.

Wonder rather than doubt is the root of knowledge. Doubt comes in the wake of knowledge as a state of vacillation between two contrary or contradictory views; as a state in which a belief we had embraced begins to totter. It challenges the mind's accounts about reality and calls for an examination and verification of that which is deposited in the mind. In other words, the business of doubt is one of auditing the mind's accounts about reality rather than a concern with reality itself; it deals with the content of perception rather than with perception itself.

11

Doubt is not applied to that which we have an immediate awareness of. We do not doubt that we exist or that we see, we merely question whether we know what we see or whether that which we see is a true reflection of what exists in reality. Thus, it is after perception has been crystallized in a conception that doubt springs up.

Doubt, then, is an interdepartmental activity of the mind. First we see, next we judge and form an opinion and thereafter we doubt. In other words, to doubt is to question that which we have accepted as possibly true a moment ago. Doubt is an act of appeal, a proceeding by which a logical judgment is brought from the memory to the critical faculty of the mind for re-examination. Accordingly, we must first judge and cling to a belief in our judgment before we are able to doubt. But if we must know in order to question, if we must entertain a belief in order to cast doubt upon it, then doubt cannot be the beginning of knowledge.

Wonder goes beyond knowledge. We do not doubt that we doubt, but we are amazed at our ability to doubt, amazed at our ability to wonder. He who is sluggish will berate doubt; he who is blind will berate wonder. Doubt may come to an end, wonder lasts forever. Wonder is a state of mind in which we do not look at reality through the latticework of our memorized knowledge; in which nothing is taken for granted. Spiritually we cannot live by merely reiterating borrowed or inherited knowledge. Inquire of your soul what does it know, what does it take for granted. It will tell you only no-thing is taken for granted; each thing is a surprise, *being is unbelievable*. We are amazed at seeing anything at all; amazed not only at particular values and things but *at the unexpectedness of being as such*, at the fact that there is being at all.

Man is not alone

A philosophy that begins with radical doubt ends in radical despair. It was the principle of *dubito ut intelligam* that prepared the soil for modern gospels of despair. "Philosophy begins in wonder" (Plato, *Theatetus* 155D), in a state of mind which we should like to call *thaumatism* (from *thaumazein*—to doubt) as distinguished from skepticism.

Even before we conceptualize what we perceive, we are amazed beyond words, beyond doubts. We may doubt anything, except that we are struck with amazement. When in doubt, we raise questions; when in wonder, we do not even know how to ask a question. Doubts may be resolved, radical amazement can never be erased. There is no answer in the world to man's radical wonder. Under the running sea of our theories and scientific explanations lies the aboriginal abyss of radical amazement.

Radical amazement has a wider scope than any other act of man. While any act of perception or cognition has as its object a selected segment of reality, radical amazement refers to all of reality; not only to what we see, but also to the very act of seeing as well as to our own selves, to the selves that see and are amazed at their ability to see.

THE MYSTERY WITHIN REASON

The ineffable is not a particular puzzle to the mind, as, for example, the cause of volcanic eruptions. We do not have to go to the end of reasoning to encounter it. The ineffable is, as we have said above, something with which we are confronted everywhere and at all times. Even the very act of thinking baffles our thinking, just as every intelligible fact is, by virtue of its being a fact, drunk with baffling aloofness. Does not mystery reign within reasoning, within perception, within explanation? Where is the self-understanding that could unfurl the marvel of our own thinking, that could explain the grace of our emptying the concrete with charms of abstraction? What formula could explain and solve the enigma of the very fact of thinking? Ours is neither thing nor thought, but only the subtle magic blending the two.

What fills us with radical amazement is not the relations in which everything is embedded but the fact that even the minimum of perception is a maximum of enigma. The most incomprehensible fact is the fact that we comprehend at all.

It is impossible to be at ease and to repose on ideas which have turned into habits, on "canned" theories, in which our own or other people's insights are preserved. We can never leave behind our concern in the safe-deposit of opinions, nor delegate its force to others and so attain vicarious insights. We must keep our own amazement, our own eagerness alive. And if we ever fail in our quest for insight, it is not because it cannot be found, but because we do not know how to live, or how to beware of the mind's narcissistic tendency to fall in love with its own reflection, a tendency which cuts thought off its roots.

The tree of knowledge and the tree of life have their roots in the same soil. But, playing with winds and beams, the tree of knowledge often grows brilliant, sapless leaves instead of fruits. Let the leaves wither, but the sap should not dry up.

Man is not alone

What is subtle speculation worth without the pristine insight into the sacredness of life, an insight which we try to translate into philosophy's rational terms, into religion's ways of living, into art's forms and visions? To maintain the stir and flow of that insight in all thoughts, so that even in our doubts its sap should not cease to flush, means to draw from the soil of what is creative in civilization and religion, a soil which only artificial flowers can dispense with.

The sense of the ineffable does not hush the quest of thought, but, on the contrary, disturbs the placid and unseals our suppressed impressionability. The approach to the ineffable leads through the depth of knowledge rather than through ignorant animal gazing. To the minds of those who do not make the universal mistake of assuming as known a world that is unknown, of placing the solution before the enigma, the abundance of the utterable can never displace the world of the ineffable.

Souls that are focused and do not falter at first sight, falling back on words and ready-made notions with which the memory is replete, can behold the mountains as if they were gestures of exaltation. To them all sight is suddenness, and eyes which do not discern the flash in the darkness of a thing perceive but series of clichés.

EXPERIENCE WITHOUT EXPRESSION

Always we are chasing words, and always words recede. But the greatest experiences are those for which we have no expression. To live only on that which we can say is to wallow in the dust, instead of digging up the soil. How shall we ignore the mystery, in which we are involved, to which we are attached by our very existence? How shall we remain deaf to the throb of the cosmic that is subtly echoed in our own souls? The most intimate is the most mysterious. Wonder alone is the compass that may direct us to the pole of meaning. As I enter the next second of my life, while writing these lines, I am aware that to be swept by the enigma and to pause —rather than to flee and to forget—is to live within the core.

To become aware of the ineffable is to part company with words. The essence, the tangent to the curve of human experience, lies beyond the limits of language. The world of things we perceive is but a veil. Its flutter is music, its ornament science, but what it conceals is inscrutable. Its silence remains unbroken; no words can carry it away.

Sometimes we wish the world could cry and tell us about that which made it pregnant with fear-filling grandeur. Sometimes we wish our own heart would speak of that which made it heavy with wonder.

THE ROOT OF REASON

Do we owe all we know to discursive thinking? Does our syllogistic power bear the whole brunt? Reasoning is not the only motor of mental life. Who does not know that more is contained in our convictions than has been crystallized in definable concepts? It is a misconception to assume that there is nothing in our consciousness that was not previously in perception or analytical reason. Much of the wisdom inherent in our consciousness is the root, rather than the fruit, of reason. There are more songs in our souls than the tongue is able to utter. When detached from its original insights, the discursive mind becomes a miser, and when we discover that concepts bring no relief to our outraged conscience and thirst for integrity, we turn to the origin of thought, to the endless shore that lies across the logical. Just as the mind is able to form conceptions supported by sense perception, it can derive insights from the dimension of the ineffable. Insights are the roots of art, philosophy and religion, and must be acknowledged as common and fundamental facts of mental life. The ways of creative thinking do not always coincide with those charted by traditional logicians; the realm where genius is at home, where insight is at work, logic can hardly find access to.

3 The World Is an Allusion

It is not in a roundabout way, by analogy or inference, that we become aware of the ineffable; we do not think about it *in absentia*. It is rather sensed as something immediately given by way of an insight that is unending and underivable, logically and psychologically prior to judgment, to the assimilation of subject matter to mental categories; a universal insight into an objective aspect of reality, of which all men are at all times capable; not the froth of ignorance but the climax of thought, indigenous to the climate that prevails at the summit of intellectual endeavor, where such works as the last quartets of Beethoven come into being. It is a cognitive insight, since the awareness it evokes is a definite addition to the mind.

A UNIVERSAL PERCEPTION

The sense of the ineffable is not an esoteric faculty but an ability with which all men are endowed; it is potentially as common as sight or as the ability to form syllogisms. For just as man is endowed with the ability to know certain aspects of reality, he is endowed with the ability to know that there is more than what he knows. His mind is concerned with the ineffable as well as with the expressible, and the awareness of his radical amazement is as universally valid as the principle of contradiction or the principle of sufficient reason.

Just as material things offer resistance to our spontaneous impulses, and it is that feeling of resistance that makes us believe that these things are real, not illusory, so does the ineffable offer resistance to our categories.

What the sense of the ineffable perceives is something *objective* which cannot be conceived by the mind nor captured by imagination or feeling, something real which, by its very essence, is beyond the reach of thought and feeling. What we are primarily aware of is not our self, our inner mood, but a transubjective situation, in regard to which our ability fails. Subjective is the *manner*, not the *matter* of our perception. What we perceive is objective in the sense of being independent of and corresponding to our perception. Our radical amazement responds to the mystery, but does not produce it. You and I have not invented the grandeur of the sky nor endowed man with the mystery of birth and death. We do not create the ineffable, we encounter it.

Our awareness of it is potentially present in every perception, every act of thinking and every enjoyment or valuation of reality. Since it is an incontestable fact, no theory of man would be complete if it were left out. It is attested to by undaunted triumphant explorers who, when they have reached the peak, are more humble than ever before.

Subjective is the absence not the presence of radical amazement. Such lack or absence is a sign of a half-hearted, listless mind, of an undeveloped sense for the depth of things.

The ineffable, therefore, may be verified by every non-sophisticated man who must come upon it in his own unmitigated experience. This is why all words that hint at the ineffable are understandable to everybody.

Without the concept of the *ineffable* it would be impossible to account for the diversity of man's attempts to express or depict reality, for the diversity of philosophies, poetic visions or artistic representations, for the consciousness that we are still at the beginning of our effort to say what we see about us.

We have characterized the perception of the ineffable as a universal perception. But if its content is not communicable, how do we know that it is the same in all men?

To this we may say that while we are unable either to define or to describe the ineffable, it is given to us to point to it. By means of *indicative* rather than descriptive terms, we are able to convey to others those features of our perception which are known to all men.

Perceptions of beauty are not expressed by definitions either, and because that which we sense is not identical in all regards, the descriptions offered are highly divergent. Yet we assume that they all mean essentially the same. This is because the reader recognizes in the descriptions the essence of a perception in which he shares, although the descriptions themselves differ widely.

The ineffable is not a synonym for the unknown or the non-descript; its essence is not in its being an enigma, in its being hidden behind the curtain.

What we encounter in our perception of the sublime, in our radical amazement, is a spiritual suggestiveness of reality, an *allusiveness* to transcendent meaning. The world in its grandeur is full of a spiritual radiance, for which we have neither name nor concept.

We are struck with an awareness of the immense preciousness of being; a preciousness which is not an object of analysis but a cause of wonder; it is inexplicable, nameless, and cannot be specified or put in one of our categories. Yet, we have a *certainty without knowledge*: it is real without being expressible. It cannot be communicated to others; every man has to find it by himself. In moments of sensing the ineffable we are as certain of the value of the world as we are of its existence. There must be a value which was worth the world's coming into existence. We may be skeptical as to whether the world is perfect. Yet, even its imperfection admitted, the preciousness of its grandeur is beyond question.

Thus, while the ineffable is a term of negation indicating a limitation of expression, its content is intensely affirmative, denoting an *allusiveness* to something meaningful, for which we possess no means of expression. Usually we regard as meaningful that which can be expressed, and as meaningless that which cannot be expressed. Yet, the equation of the meaningful and the expressible ignores a vast realm of human experience, and

22

is refuted by our sense of the ineffable which is an awareness of an allusiveness to meaning without the ability to express it. That the sense of the ineffable is an awareness of meaning is indicated by the fact that the inner response it evokes is that of awe or reverence.

4 To Be Is to Stand For

THE UNIVERSALITY OF REVERENCE

Reverence is an attitude as indigenous to human consciousness as fear when facing danger or pain when hurt. The scope of revered objects may vary, reverence itself is characteristic of man in all civilizatións. Let us analyze a rather common and perhaps universal example of such an attitude, the inner structure of which will prove to be the same in all examples—whatever the object revered may be. Obviously, we can never sneer at the stars, mock the dawn or scoff at the totality of being. Sublime grandeur evokes unhesitating, unflinching awe. Away from the immense, cloistered in our own concepts, we may scorn and revile everything. But standing between earth and sky, we are silenced by the sight. . . .

Why is it impossible to be overbearing in the face of the universe? Is it because of fear? The stars could do us no harm, if we ridiculed them. Is it because of a fear inherited from our primitive ancestors, an atavistic superstition that should be discarded? No one who is unprejudiced is able in the presence of grandeur to declare that such reverence is fatuous or absurd. Is it a higher form of egotism? No sane person could cherish the desire to venerate himself. Reverence is always for someone else; there is no self-reverence.

Ignorance is not the cause of reverence. The unknown as such does not fill us with awe. We have no feelings of awe for the other side of the moon or for that which will happen tomorrow. Nor is it might or mass that arouses such an attitude. It is not the prize-fighter or the millionaire but the fragile old man or our mother whom we find venerable. Nor do we revere an object for its beauty, a statement for its logical consistency or an institution for its purposefulness.

Nor do we ever revere the known; because the known is in our grasp, and we revere only that which surpasses us. We do not revere the regularity of the year's seasons, but that which makes it possible; not the calculating machine, but the mind that invented it; not the sun, but the power that created it. It is the *extremely precious*, morally, intellectually or spiritually, that we revere.

Reverence is one of man's answers to the presence of the mystery. This is why, in contradistinction to other emotions, it does not rush to be spoken. When we stand in awe, our lips do not demand speech, knowing that if we spoke, we would deprave ourselves. In such moments talk is an abomination. All we want is to pause, to be still, that the moment may last. It is like listening to great music; how it reaps the yield from the fertile soil of stillness; we are swept by it without being able to appraise it. The meaning of the things we revere is overwhelming and beyond the grasp of our understanding. We possess no categories for it and would distort it if we tried to appraise it by our standard of values; it essentially surpasses our criteria.

Man is not alone

The objection may be voiced that a psychological reaction is no evidence for an ontological fact, and we can never infer an object itself from a feeling a person has about it. The feeling of awe may often be the result of a misunderstanding of an ordinary fact; one may be overawed by an artificial spectacle or a display of evil power. That objection is, of course, valid. Yet what we infer from is not the actual feeling of awe but the intellectual certainty that in the face of nature's grandeur and mystery we must respond with awe; what we infer from is not a psychological state but a fundamental norm of human consciousness, a *categorical imperative*. Indeed, the validity and requiredness of awe enjoy a degree of certainty that is not even surpassed by the axiomatic certainty of geometry.

We do not sense the mystery because we feel a need for it, just as we do not notice the ocean or the sky because we have a desire to see them. The sense of mystery is not a product of our will. It may be suppressed by the will but it is not generated by it. The mystery is not the product of a need, it is a fact.

That sweep of mystery is not a thought in our mind but a most powerful presence beyond the mind. In asserting that the ineffable is spiritually real, independent of our perception, we do not endow a mere idea with existence, just as I do not do so in asserting: "This is an ocean," when I am carried away by its waves. The ineffable is there before we form an idea of it. To the spirit of man his own spirit is a reliable witness that the mystery is not an absurdity, that, on the contrary, things

27

known and perceptible are charged with its heart-stripping, galvanizing meaning.

Our assumption that there is meaning in things which has the quality of inspiring the human mind with awe implies a principle that may come as a surprise to many readers; namely, that meaning is something which occurs *outside the mind* in objective things—independent of subjective awareness of it. We do, indeed, claim that meanings, just as facts, are independent of the structure of the human mind and given with or within things and events. In abstract analysis we distinguish and divide between fact and meaning, yet in actual perception they are given together. There are no naked, neutral facts. Being as such is inconceivable; it is always endowed with meaning.

Meaning is not man's gift to reality. To assume that reality is chaotic, bare of significance, as long as man does not approach it with the magic touch of his mind, would be to deny that nature behaves according to law. The essence of thought is discovery rather than invention.

In the common man's perception facts appear with a minimum of significance, while to the artist the fact overflows with meaning; things communicate to him more significance than he is able to absorb. Creative living in art, science and religion is a denial of the assumption that man is the source of significance; he merely lends his categories and means of expression to a meaning which is there. Only those who have lost their

28

sense of meaning would claim that self-expression rather than world-expression is the purpose of living.

EXPECTEDNESS AND CERTAINTY OF MEANING

Expectedness of meaning, the certainty that whatever exists must be worth while, that whatever is real must be compatible with a thought, is at the root of all our thinking, feeling and volition. It is reason's oracle or axiom, on its vindication we stake all we possess, and there is no refuge from it but self-slaughter and the will to madness. Always looking for some intrinsic quality in reality that would exhibit its significance, we are sure that the hidden and unknown will never turn out to be absurd or meaningless. There is a transcendent *preciousness* that surpasses our power of appreciation, and of which our highest values are but a faint indication. The world is resplendent with such preciousness; we sense it wherever we go, with our hearts too feeble or unworthy to fathom it.

Should we condemn that certainty as a wild audacity, since it fails to be constantly vindicated? Or is it our mind which is to be blamed for misunderstanding its own expectation, for its compromising with some of its vagaries and eccentric notions, thus distorting what was originally an authentic insight? The notion that supreme meaning must be self-advertising like a clock, the tendency to fling favorite anthropocentric conceptions at the world, have made a caricature of mystery. The scandal of trying to adapt meaning to our minds, of constantly seeking what is the universe worth to us, may, indeed, seal the doom of our understanding of meaning.

Science does not try to fathom the mystery. It merely describes and explains the way in which things behave in terms of causal necessity. It does not try to give us an explanation in terms of logical necessity—why things *must* be at all, and why the laws of nature *must* be the way they are. We do not know, for example, *why* certain combinations of a definite kind form a constellation which goes with the phenomena of electricity, while others with the phenomena of magnetism. The knowledge of how the world functions gives us neither an acquaintance with its essence nor an insight into its meaning, just as the knowledge of general physiology and psychology does not give us an acquaintance with the Dalai Lama whom we have never met.

Trying to pierce the mystery with our categories is like trying to bite a wall. Science extends rather than limits the scope of the ineffable, and our radical amazement is enhanced rather than reduced by the advancement of knowledge. The theory of evolution and adaptation of the species does not disenchant the organism of its wonder. Men like Kepler and Newton who have stood face to face with the reality of the infinite would have been unable to coin a phrase about the heavens declaring the glory not of God, but of Kepler and Newton; or the verse: "Glory to man in the highest! for man is the master of things."

Scientific research is an entry into the endless, not a blind alley; solving one problem, a greater one enters our sight. One answer breeds a multitude of new questions; explanations are

30

merely indications of greater puzzles. Everything hints at something that transcends it; the detail indicates the whole, the whole, its idea, the idea, its mysterious root. What appears to be a center is but a point on the periphery of another center. The totality of a thing is actual infinity.

ALL KNOWLEDGE IS A PARTICLE

There is no true thinker who does not possess an awareness that his thought is a part of an endless context, that his ideas are not taken from the air. All philosophy is but a word in a sentence, just as to a composer the most complete symphony is but a note in an inexhaustible melody. Only when intoxicated with our own ideas do we consider the world of spirit a soliloquy; ideals, thoughts, melodies our own shadows. The rich in spirit do not know how to be proud of what they grasp, for they sense that the things which they comprehend are outbursts of inconceivable significance, that there are no lonely ideas roaming about in a void, to be seized and appropriated. *To be* implies to *stand for*, because every being is representative of something that is more than itself; because the seen, the known, stands for the unseen, the unknown. Even the most abstract mathematical formula to which we may reduce the order of the universe arouses the question: What does it signify? The answer will necessarily be: It represents the majesty of that which is more than itself. At whatever climax of thinking we may arrive, we face transcendent significance.

The world's mystery is either chaos without value of any kind, or is replete with an infinite significance beyond the reach of finite minds; in other words, it is either absolutely meaningless or absolutely meaningful, either too inferior or too superior to be an object of human comprehension.

Yet, how would we know of the mystery of being if not through our sense of the ineffable, and it is this sense that communicates to us the supremacy and grandeur of the ineffable together with the knowledge of its reality. Thus, we cannot deny the superiority of the ineffable to our minds, although, for the same reason, we cannot prove it.

On the other hand, the fact of our being able to sense it and to be aware of its existence at all is a sure indication that the ineffable stands in some relationship to the mind of man. We should, therefore, not label it as *irrational*, to be disregarded as the residue of knowledge, as dreary remains of speculation unworthy of our attention. The ineffable is conceivable in spite of its being unknowable.

IS THE INEFFABLE AN ILLUSION?

Against our affirmation of the ineffable the following argument may be raised: Granted that certain meaning-qualities are given within reality, there are certainly other meaning-qualities which, while we take them to be real, are mere illusions. We do not claim, for example, that there is something in reality that corresponds to the grotesque images of demons worshiped in primitive religious cults. Is not the ineffable, too, a mere word, a sham? Does its being meaningful to us necessarily prove that there is something for which it stands? What is the guarantee that the awareness of the ineffable is

32

more than a subjective impression? Let us accept a theory and say it is a dream that grows at the mind's frontier, the magical offspring of intense but wishful thinking! Yet the smooth and elegant way which this theory offers is deceptive; it is, in fact, too slippery to walk on. Why in the world should man desire or postulate a marvel that he can neither master nor grasp, that fills him with terror and humility? Theories are always magnanimous, but their test comes when applied. Is it imaginable that an international academy of scholars should one day proclaim: there is nothing to revere; the mystery of life, of heaven and earth, is but a figment of the mind?

To assert that the most sensitive minds of all ages were victims of an illusion; that religion, poetry, art, philosophy were the outcome of a self-deception is too sophisticated to be reasonable. Bringing discredit on the genius of man, such an assertion would, of course, disqualify our own minds for making any assertion. It is true that the history of religion abounds in examples of idols and symbols that had meaning to certain people but were meaningless to others. But did they really stand for nothing? We can point to psychical complexes which have presumably affected the desire to produce those primitive idols as well as to their ludicrousness and perversity. Yet, rejecting them as willful products of the mind does not vitiate the sense of mystery implicit in the urge to produce and worship them. The idol-worshipper's error begins in the process of expressing his sense of mystery, when he begins to relate the transcendent to his conventional needs and ideas and tries to specify that which is beyond his grasp. In that process motives come into play that have nothing to do with his original insight. He begins to regard the instrumental as final, the temporal as ultimate, thus distorting both the facts he adores as well as the quality of the divine he is bestowing upon them. He still has to hear: "Thou shalt not make unto thee a graven image, nor any manner of likeness." No thing can serve as a symbol or likeness of God—not even the universe.

On a lovely summer afternoon an influential educator admired the sky. His little girl turned and asked: "What is there beyond the sky?" The father gave her a "scientific" answer: "Ether, my child." Whereupon the girl exclaimed: "Ether!" and she held her nose . . .

5 Knowledge by Appreciation

A PERCEPTION AT THE END OF PERCEPTION

We are rarely aware of the tangent of the beyond at the whirling wheel of experience. In our passion for knowledge, our minds prey upon the wealth of an unresisting world and, seizing our limited spoils, we quickly leave the ground to lose ourselves in the whirlwind of our own knowledge.

The horizon of knowledge is lost in the mist produced by fads and phrases. We refuse to take notice of what is beyond our sight, content with converting realities into opinions, mysteries into dogmas and ideas into a multitude of words. What is extraordinary appears to us as habit, the dawn a daily routine of nature. But time and again we awake. In the midst of walking in the never-ending procession of days and nights, we are suddenly filled with a solemn terror, with a feeling of our wisdom being inferior to dust. We cannot endure the heartbreaking splendor of sunsets. Of what avail, then, are opinions, words, dogmas? In the confinement of our study rooms, our knowledge seems to us a pillar of light. But when we stand at the door which opens out to the infinite, we realize that all concepts are but glittering motes that populate a sunbeam.

To some of us explanations and opinions are tokens of the wonder's departure, like a curfew ringing the end of insight and search. However, those to whom reality is dearer than information, to whom life is stronger than concepts and the world more than words, are never deluded into believing that what they know and perceive is the core of reality. We are able to exploit, to label things with well-trimmed words; but when ceasing to subject them to our purposes and to impose on them the forms of our intellect, we are stunned and incapable of saying what things are in themselves; it is an experience of being unable to experience something we face: too great to be perceived. Music, poetry, religion—they all initiate in the soul's encounter with an aspect of reality for which reason has no concepts and language has no names.

THE WAY OF EXPEDIENCY

Most of our attention is given to the expedient, to that which is conducive to our advantage and which would enable us to exploit the resources of our planet. If our philosophy were a projection of man's actual behavior, we would have to define the value of the earth as a source of supply for our industries, and the ocean as a fishpond. However, as we have seen, there is more than one aspect of nature that commands our attention. We go out to meet the world not only by way of expediency but also by the way of wonder. In the first we accumulate information in order to dominate; in the second we deepen our appreciation in order to respond. Power is the language of expediency; poetry the language of wonder.

Man is not alone

When seeking to expand our knowledge for the sake of gratifying our passion for power, the world turns out to be alien and weird; while the knowledge we acquire in our yearning to invoke appreciation is a way of discovering our unison with things. With information we are alone; in appreciation we are with all things.

THE WILL TO WONDER

As civilization advances, the sense of wonder almost necessarily declines. Such decline is an alarming symptom of our state of mind. Mankind will not perish for want of information; but only for want of appreciation. The beginning of our happiness lies in the understanding that life without wonder is not worth living. What we lack is not a will to believe but a will to wonder.

To intercept the allusions that are submerged in perceptibilities, the interstitial values that never rise to the surface, the indefinable dimension of all existence, is the venture of true poetry. This is why poetry is to religion what analysis is to science, and it is certainly no accident that the Bible was not written *more geometrico* but in the language of poets. However, the ineffable as sensed by the artist is anonymous, it is like a foundling. To the religious man nothing is ever deserted or unclaimed; it is as if God stood between him and the world. The most familiar retires from his sight, and he discerns the original beneath the palimpsests of things.

Our self-assured mind specializes in producing knives, as if it were a cutlery, and in all its thoughts it flings a blade, cutting the world in two: in a thing and in a self; in an object and in a subject that conceives the object as distinct from itself. A mercenary of our will to power, the mind is trained to assail in order to plunder rather than to commune in order to love. Moreover, selective as our attention necessarily is, beholding one thing, we overlook all others which, being out of control, set our authority at naught.

When ceasing to convert the world into objects of our abstraction, man comes to realize that he is treated like a satellite by his own mind, which keeps him from getting in touch with reality itself and never gives its own secret away, debarring him from the essence rather than initiating him into it.

Where man meets the world, not with the tools he has made but with the soul with which he was born; not like a hunter who seeks his prey but like a lover to reciprocate love; where man and matter meet as equals before the mystery, both made, maintained and destined to pass away, it is not an object, a thing that is given to his sense, but a state of fellowship that embraces him and all things; not a particular fact but the startling situation that there are facts at all; being; the presence of a universe; the unfolding of time. The sense of the ineffable does not stand between man and mystery; rather than shutting him out of it, it brings him together with it.

Man is not alone

To our knowledge the world and the "I" are two, an object and a subject; but *within* our wonder the world and the "I" are one in being, in eternity. We become alive to our living in the great fellowship of all beings, we cease to regard things as opportunities to exploit. Conformity to the ego is no longer our exclusive concern, and our right to harness reality in the service of so-called practical ends becomes a problem.

Things surrounding us emerge from the triteness with which we have endowed them, and their strangeness opens like a void between them and our mind, a void that no words can fill. How does it happen that I am using this pen and writing these lines? Who are we to scan the esoteric stars, to witness the settings of the sun, to have the service of the spring for our survival? How shall we ever reciprocate for breathing and thinking, for sight and hearing, for love and achievement? Some prolonged, mind-piercing evidence weans us then from mistaking the benignity of the world for ownerlessness, its symbolic living for dull order.

One of the greatest shocks that we experience in our childhood comes with the discovery that our needs and deeds are not always approved by our fellow-men, that the world is not mere food for our delight. The resistance we encounter, the refusals we incur, open our eyes to the existence of a world outside ourselves. But growing older and stronger, we gradually recover from that shock, try to forget its dolorous lesson and apply most of our ingenuity to enforcing our will on nature and men. No recollection of our past experience completely upsets the arrogance that time and again jams the traffic in our mind. Dazzled by the brilliant achievements of the intellect in science and technique, we have been deluded into believing that we are the masters of the earth and our will the ultimate criterion of what is right and wrong.

IS THE WORLD AT THE MERCY OF MAN?

We are today beginning to awake from a state of intoxication, from a juvenile happiness with the triumphs of our wisdom. We are beginning to realize in what a sad plight both nature and man would be if they were completely at the mercy of man and his vagaries. We must not be deceived by the limited splendor of theories that answer none of our most vital problems and only ridicule the inborn urge to ask the most crying, urgent question: What is the secret of existence? Wherefore and for whose sake do we live? Only those who have not tasted the terror of life, only those who claim that it is a pleasure to live and that more and only pleasure is in store for the generations to come, can deny the essential necessity of asking: Wherefore? For whose sake?

WE SING FOR ALL THINGS

The practical mind pays more attention to the commas and colons in the great text of reality than to its content and meaning, while to the sense of the ineffable things stand out like marks of exclamation, like silent witnesses; and the soul of man is an urge to sing for all beings about that for which they all stand. All things carry a surplus of meaning over being—they mean more than what they are in themselves. Even finite facts stand for infinite meaning. It is as if all things were vibrant with spiritual meaning, and all we try to do in creative art and in good deeds is to intone the secret strain, an aspect of that meaning.

As long as we see only objects we are alone. When we begin to sing, we sing for all things. Essentially music does not describe that which is, rather it tries to convey that which reality stands for. The universe is a score of eternal music, and we are the cry, we are the voice.

Reason explores the laws of nature, trying to decipher the scales without grasping the harmony, while the sense of the ineffable is in search of the song. When we think, we employ words or symbols of what we feel about things. When we sing, we are carried away by our wonder; and *acts of wonder* are signs or symbols of what all things stand for.

6 A Question beyond Words

The universe is an immense allusion, and our inner life an anonymous quotation; only the italics are our own. Is it within our power to verify the quotation, to identify the source, to learn what all things stand for?

The question is the beginning of all thinking. In knowing how to ask the right question lies the only hope of arriving at an answer. In asking a question we must faintly anticipate something of the nature of what we ask about. On that account, the question about the ultimate source of all reality is one we do not know how to ask. It concerns something which cannot be pressed into our finite categories, put in chains of a sentence and converted into a definite matter to be inquired into. Formulas—such as: What is the ultimate origin of the universe? What is behind all events?—are travesties of what is overwhelmingly given to our pristine sense of wonder. Is it the origin we want to ask about and not the presence, goal and task of the universe? Do we know where to draw the line between the unknown origin and the known product, or where the source ends and the derivation begins? Even the sentence structure of such formulas is pregnant with logical assumptions which upon close analysis disclose immense difficulties.

A profound awareness of the incongruity of all categories with the nameless, unfathomable omnipresence of the mystery is a prerequisite for our efforts in reaching toward an answer. The more we beware of letting our incomparable question be adulterated or even stifled by inadequate formulations, the better will be our chance of braving final, specious answers.

WHEREFORE? FOR WHOSE SAKE?

For in our anxiety, all caution and prudence are forgotten. Neither sage nor savage is able to circumvent the problem: Who is the great author? Why is there a world at all? What is the sense of being alive?

Despite our conquests and might, we are like blind beggars in a labyrinth who do not know at which door to knock to obtain relief for our anxieties. We know *how* nature acts but not *why* and *for whose sake;* we know that we live but not why and wherefore. We know that we must inquire but not who has planted in us the anxiety to inquire.

Intimidated by the vigor of agnosticism that proclaims ignorance about the ultimate as the only honest attitude, modern man shies away from metaphysics and is inclined to suppress his innate sense, to crush his mind-transcending questions and to seek refuge within the confines of his finite self. Yet such an attitude is a trap, both inconsistent and self-deceptive. In insisting that we are unable to know, we exhibit a knowledge which we claim is unattainable. The allegation that there is no ultimate meaning sounds shrilly in the deep stillness of the ineffable.

Is it possible to evade the ultimate issue by withdrawing within the confines of the self? The awareness of wonder is often overtaken by the mind's tendency to dichotomize, which makes us look at the ineffable as if it were a thing or an aspect of things apart from our own selves; as if only the stars were surrounded with a halo of enigma and not our own existence. The truth is that the self, our "lord," is an unknown thing, inconceivable in itself. In penetrating the self, we discover the paradox of not knowing what we presume to know so well.

WHO IS "I"?

Man sees the things that surround him long before he becomes aware of his own self. Many of us are conscious of the hiddenness of things, but few of us sense the mystery of our own presence. The self cannot be described in the terms of the mind, for all our symbols are too poor to render it. The self is more than we dream of; it stands, as it were, with its back to the mind. Indeed, to the mind even the mind itself is more enigmatic than a star. Elusive is the manner in which the human mind operates; the ideas, the bricks of which convictions are made, are symbols the meaning of which man never fully penetrates, and what he wishes to express is submerged in the unfathomable depth of the unconscious. Beyond my reach is the bottom of my own inner life. I am not even sure whether it is the voice of a definite personal unit that comes out of me. What in my voice has originated in me and what is the resonance of transsubjective reality? In saying "I," my intention is to differentiate myself from other people and other things. But what is the direct, positive content of the "I": the blooming of consciousness upon the impenetrable soil of the subconscious? The self comprises no less unknown, subconscious, than known, conscious reality. This means that the self can be distinctly separated only at its branches; namely, from other individuals and other things but not at its roots.

All we know of the self is its expression, but the self is never fully expressed. What we are, we cannot say; what we become, we cannot grasp. It is all a cryptic, suggestive abbreviation which the mind tries in vain to decipher. Like the burning bush, the self is aflame but is never consumed. Carrying within itself more than reason, it is in travail with the ineffable. Something is meant by the simile of man. But what?

As we shall see,* to exist implies to own time. But does a man own time? The fact is that time, the moments through which I live, I cannot own, while the timeless in my temporality is certainly not my private property. However, if life does not belong exclusively to me, what is my legal title to it? Does my essence possess the right to say "I"? Who is that "I" to whom my life is supposed to belong? Nobody knows either its content or its limits. Is it something that withers or is it something that time cannot take away?

As an individual, as an "I," I am separated from external reality, from other men and other things. But in the only

* Compare p. 200.

relation in which the "I" becomes aware of itself, in the relation to existence, I find that what I call "self" is a self-deception; that existence is not a property but a trust; that the self is not an isolated entity, confined in itself, a kingdom ruled by our will.

What we face in penetrating the self is the paradox of not knowing what we presume to know so well. Once we discover that the self in itself is a monstrous deceit, that the self is something transcendent in disguise, we begin to feel the pressure that keeps us down to a mere self. We begin to realize that our normal consciousness is in a state of trance, that what is higher in us is usually suspended. We begin to feel like strangers within our normal consciousness, as if our own will were imposed on us.

Clear-sighted souls, caught in the tension of the lavishly obvious and the clandestine stillness, are neither dazzled nor surprised. Watching the never-ending pantomime that goes on within an ostentatious, turbulent world, they know that the mystery is not there, while we are here. The truth is we are all steeped in it, imbued with it; we are, partly, it.

I AM THAT I AM NOT

> And God said unto Moses:
> I Am that I Am, and He said:
> Thus shalt thou say to the children of Israel,
> I Am hath sent me unto you.
>
> (Exodus 3:14)

I am endowed with a will, but the will is not mine; I am endowed with freedom, but it is a freedom imposed on the will. Life is something that visits my body, a transcendent loan; I have neither initiated nor conceived its worth and meaning. The essence of what I am is not mine. *I am what is not mine.* I am that I am not.

Upon the level of normal consciousness I find myself wrapt in self-consciousness and claim that my acts and states originate in and belong to myself. But in penetrating and exposing the self, I realize that the self did not originate in itself, that the essence of the self is in its being a non-self, that ultimately man is not a subject but an *object.**

NO SUBJECT TO ASK

It is easy to raise verbally the question: Who is the subject, of which my self is the object? But to be keenly sensitive to its meaning is something which surpasses our power of comprehension. It is, in fact, impossible to comprehend logically its implications. For in asking the question, I am always aware of the fact that it is I who asks the question. But as soon as I know myself as an "I," as a subject, I am not capable any more of grasping the content of the question, in which I am posited as an object. Thus, on the level of self-consciousness there is no way to face the issue, to ask the absolute question. On the other hand, when we are overtaken with the spirit of the ineffable, there is no logical self left to ask the question or the mental power to stand as the judge with God as an object, about the existence of whom I am to decide. I am

* See p. 128.

unable to raise my voice or to sit in judgment. There is no self to say: I think that . . .

There is, indeed, no speculative level where the question could be raised. We either do not sense the meaning of the issue or, when realizing what we ought to ask about, there is no logical subject left to ask, to examine, to inquire.

7 The God of Philosophers

Traditionally the ultimate question is phrased in terms of speculation. Taking as its point of departure the world or the order of nature, we would ask: Do the facts of this world suggest the presence or existence of a supreme intelligence?

Science is based upon the assumption that there are intelligible laws in nature which can be observed, conceived and described by the human mind. The scientist did not invent these intricate laws; they were there long before he set about to explore them. In whatever way, then, we try to conceive the reality of nature—as a mechanism or as an organic order —it is given to us as a meaningful whole, the processes of which are ruled by strict principles. These principles are not only inherent in the actual relations between the components of reality, they are also intrinsically rational if our minds are capable of grasping them.

But if rationality is at work in nature, there is no way to account for it without reference to the activity of a supreme intelligence.

51

The probability, therefore, that the universe came into being without design is infinitesimally slight, while the probability that intelligence is at the root of being is so strong that not even the foundation of science enjoys a greater likelihood. The coming about of the universal order by sheer accident—which is an irrational category—appears far less plausible to our minds than its coming about at the hand of a superrational designer.

It is a matter of no great difficulty to discover some subtle fallacies in the speculative proofs. It may be said, for example, that the presence of order in the world does not prove the existence of a divine mind which is above and apart from that order. From order we may only infer the existence of a higher cause, but not the existence of a being which transcends all causality. Or, to put it logically, the universe as conceived by us is a closed system of logical relations, and all we may infer from it is an ultimate logical structure. By assuming the existence of an ultimate mind or being beyond the universe, we pass from the realm of logic to that of ontology. Logically, it may be claimed, there is no justification for assuming the existence of an ultimate being. What we may observe in nature is a mechanical order, not a living consciousness. Consequently, all the human mind may assume is the existence of an ultimate mechanical force, a blind power of fate. As philosophers, therefore, we abstain from believing in the existence of a supreme being endowed with will and intelligence.

Such abstention is fully in keeping with our habits. We behave as if nature were like a tree lashing out of an unmarked primordial grave and we, men, are alive by mistake, by chance or by an oversight.

The world is treated by us like a mighty oak, from which

children lop off twigs and boughs, while tourists carve their names into its bark.

The speculative arguments are either cosmocentric or anthropocentric. To the cosmological argument for the existence of God, the design and reality of the universe are the point of departure. Its question is: What is the ultimate cause of all that exists? The principle of causality serves as the ladder on which the mind climbs up to a supreme being; He is looked for as an explanation for natural events, as a scientific solution to a problem. Similarly, Kant's moral argument for the existence of God starts from moral premises. If morality is to be more than an empty dream, the union of virtue and happiness must be realized. Now, experience shows abundantly that in the empirically known system of nature there is no dependence of happiness on virtue. The union must therefore be effected for us by a supreme power, not by us. Thus, it becomes a postulate of morality that there is an absolutely wise and holy supreme being.

The essential weakness of these arguments lies in the fact that their point of departure is not a religious but a cosmological or an anthropological problem. But there is also a unique religious situation, in which the mind is primarily concerned not with the problems of nature and man—urgent and important as they are—but with God; not with the relation of the world to our categories but with the relation of the world to God.

Another deficiency of the speculative proofs for the existence of God lies in the fact that even if their validity should be beyond dispute, they prove too little. What is the gist of these proofs? It is the claim that given certain facts of experience, such as the rational order of the universe, God is the necessary hypothesis to explain them. Since a conclusion cannot contain more than what the premises imply, a god derived from speculation is at best as much as our finite knowledge of the facts of the universe would demand, namely a hypothesis. From a rational justification of our creed, we may gain the idea that the existence of God is as probable as ether in physics or phlogiston in chemistry, a hypothesis that can easily be refuted or rendered superfluous by a change of premises. Furthermore, granted that the existence of a being endowed with supreme genius and wisdom has been demonstrated, the question remains: Why should we, poor creatures, be concerned about Him, the most perfect? We may, indeed, accept the idea that there is a supreme designer and still say: "So what?" As long as a concept of God does not overpower us, as long as we can say: "So what?"—it is not God that we talk about but something else.

The idea of a supreme designer may serve as a source of intellectual security in our search for the design, law and order of the universe, giving us a guarantee for the validity of scientific theory. However, the universe may be accepted as a stroke of genius, the stars as brilliant with significance, and yet our souls would not cease to be haunted by a fear of futility, a

54

fear that could not be overcome by a belief that, somewhere in
the infinite recesses of the Divinity, there is a well of wisdom.
Is it order that matters supremely? Is order the utmost that
divine wisdom could produce? We are more anxious to know
whether there is a God of justice than to learn whether there is a
God of order. Is there a God who collects the tears, who honors hope and rewards the ordeals of the guiltless? Or should
we assume that the empires of thought, the saintly goals, the
harmonies and sacrificial deeds of the honest and the meek are
nothing but images painted upon the surface of an ocean?

PHILOSOPHY OF RELIGION

The issue which philosophy of religion has to discuss first is
not belief, ritual or the religious experience, but the source of
all these phenomena: the total situation of man; not what or
how he experiences the supernatural, but why he experiences
and accepts it. The question is: What necessitates religion in
my life and in yours?

Philosophy of religion is not philosophy of a philosophy, the
philosophy of a doctrine, the interpretations of a dogma, but
the philosophy of concrete events, acts, insights, of that which
is immediately given with the pious man. The dogmas are
merely a catalogue, an indispensable index. For religion is more
than a creed or an ideology and cannot be understood when
detached from actual living. It comes to light in moments in
which one's soul is shaken with unmitigated concern about
the meaning of all meaning, about one's ultimate commitment
which is part of his very existence; in moments, in which all

foregone conclusions, all life-stifling trivialities are suspended; in which the soul is starved for an inkling of eternal reality; in moments of discerning the indestructibly sudden within the perishably constant.

There is much we can achieve in our quest of God by applying rational methods, provided we remember that, in matters that concern the totality of life, all higher attainments of our personality should be brought into play, particularly our sense of the ineffable.

8 The Ultimate Question

The speculative proofs are the result of what man does with his reason. But speculation, as we know, is not our only source of certainty. However precious the helping hand, the vital guidance and the sobering stress of reason, it does not ease the pensive burden which the world is forcing us to bear, the compulsion to care for things not convertible into mental effigies. There is, indeed, another kind of evidence for what God is and means. It is the result of what man does with his ultimate wonder, with his sense of the ineffable.

Mankind could never have brought forth the endless stream of its God-awareness out of the rock of finite facts by analyzing the design of its geological layers. Indeed, when we go beyond analysis, trying to see the rock as a rock and to ponder on what it means *to be*, it turns away its face from our scrutinies, and what remains is more unlikely, more unbelievable, than the mysterious ground of being. Then it dawns upon us that the world of the known is a world unknown, except in its functional outposts; that to entertain the notion, as if life were lucid and familiar, would be to welter in a fairy tale.

To a mind unwarped by intellectual habit, unbiased by what it already knows; to unmitigated innate surprise, there are no axioms, no dogmas; there is only wonder, the realization that the world is too incredible, too meaningful for us. The existence of the world is the most unlikely, the most unbelievable fact. Even our ability for surprise is beyond expectation. In our unmitigated wonder, we are like spirits who have never been conscious of outside reality, and to whom the knowledge of the existence of the universe has been brought for the first time. Who could believe it? Who could conceive it? We must learn to overcome the sleek certainty and learn to understand that the existence of the universe is contrary to all reasonable expectations. The mystery is where we start from without presuppositions, without allegations, without doctrines, without dogmas.

RELIGION BEGINS WITH THE SENSE OF THE INEFFABLE

Thinking about God begins at the mind's rugged shore, where the murmur breaks off abruptly, where we do not know any more how to yearn, how to be in awe. Only those who know how to live spiritually on edge will be able to go beyond the shore without longing for the certainties established on the artificial rock of our speculation.

Not theoretical speculation but the sense of the ineffable precipitates the problem of all problems. Not the apparent but the hidden in the apparent; not the wisdom but the mystery of the design of the universe; the questions we do not know how to ask have always poured oil on the flames of man's anxiety.

Man is not alone

Religion begins with the sense of the ineffable, with the awareness of a reality that discredits our wisdom, that shatters our concepts. It is, therefore, the ineffable with which we must begin, since otherwise there is no problem; and it is its perception to which we must return since otherwise no solution will be relevant.

THE ULTIMATE QUESTION

There is a noxious error which often plays havoc with philosophical endeavors in dealing with our problem. We seem to forget that a legitimate question represents more than what it says. Just as nature abhors a vacuum, so does vacuity of thought abhor problems. To be able to inquire, to look for an answer, one must be in possession of some knowledge, one must know what to look for. There must be a situation which accounts for its coming into being, a *raison d'être* for the presence of the question in the mind. Our first task, therefore, is to follow the trail to the origin of the question, to recover the knowledge it left behind. Unless our hearts are open to what is behind its verbal appearance, the question will pass us with averted face.

The realm of the ineffable rather than speculation is the climate in which the ultimate question comes into being, and it is in its natural abode, where the mystery is within reach of all thoughts, that the question must be studied. In its native state the ultimate question is different in form from the logical contour to which it is trimmed when brought to the abstract level of speculation.

There is a world where wonder is dead, where the ultimate question is out of reach. The realm of speculation where we usually debate the merit of our question is a far cry from its native abode, from the realm of the ineffable. By the time the question is placed before our critical eyes, it has withered like a leaf in the breath of an oven.

The growing sense of the ineffable that reaches and curves toward the light of an ultimate reality can never be transplanted into the shallowness of mere reflection. Torn out of its medium, it is usually metamorphosed like a rose pressed between the pages of a book. When reduced to terms and definitions, it is little more than a desiccated remnant of a once living reality.

If, nevertheless, we attempt to ponder about the ultimate question in its logical form, we should at least treat it like a plant which is uprooted from its soil, removed from its native winds, sunrays and terrestrial environment and can survive only if kept in conditions that somewhat resemble its original climate. This is why, even when our thinking about it takes place on a discursive level, our memory must remain moored to our perceptions of the ineffable, and our mind abide in a state of awe without which we never acquire a common language with the spirit of the question, without which the original nature of the problem will not disclose itself to us.

The issue at stake will be apprehended only by those who are able to find categories that mix with the unalloyed and to forge the imponderable into unique expression. It is not enough to describe the given content of the consciousness of the ineffable. We have to press the soul with questions, compelling it to understand and unravel the meaning of what is taking place as it stands at the ultimate horizon. While pene-

60

trating the consciousness of the ineffable, we may conceive the reality behind it.

Our point of departure is not the sight of the shrouded and inscrutable; from the endless mist of the unknown we would, indeed, be unable to derive an understanding of the known. It is the tension of the known and the unknown, of the common and the holy, of the nimble and the ineffable, that fills the moments of our insights.

We do not owe our ultimate question to stumbling in a mist of ignorance upon a wall of inscrutable riddles. We do not ask because of our being poor in spirit and bereft of knowledge; we ask because we sense a spirit which surpasses our ability to comprehend it. We owe our question not to something less but to something which is more than the known. We ask because the world is too much for us, because the known is crammed with marvel, because the world is replete with what is more than the world as we understand it.

The question about God is not a question about all things, but a question of all things; not an inquiry into the unknown but an inquiry into that which all things stand for; a question we ask for all things. It is phrased not in categories of reason but in *acts* in which we are astir beyond words. The mind does not know how to phrase it, yet the soul sighs it, sings it, pleads it.

In trying to solve a rational problem, we must first test what is given to our mind and what the mind's categories are able to convey. In our case, too, we must apply all we know about what is given to man's higher incomprehension, to his naked wonder, and what the intuition of the ineffable conveys to our consciousness. Let us remember the fundamental fact of a universal nondiscursive perception of the ineffable which is a sense of a transcendent meaning, of an awareness that something is meant by the universe which surpasses our power of comprehension.

Rational knowledge always involves alogical elements, such as an initial trust in the veracity of our faculties and a continual trust, a kind of faith, in the most reasonable hypothesis. In the perception of the ineffable we are forced into a faith in undisclosed meaning and are deprived of the power to disregard the unregarded. The question arises whether here, too, it is a reasonable hypothesis to which the mind is naturally drawn or for which it is craving.

True, it is the reasonable as such for which the mind craves and to which it is drawn. But the pleasure and essence of the reasonable or meaningful lie in its consistency with our minds. When we say something is reasonable, we imply that it is reasonable to us and can be integrated in our system of concepts. The ineffable, however, is meaningful without being reasonable; it neither bends to analysis nor conforms to our categories, as if it were out of place in our brains. It is, moreover, not an idea gained through abstractions, but one apprehended in the concrete and with immediacy; one, furthermore, not applied like a general law to particular phenomena, but something unembodied, a relatedness, surpassing the facts rather than being within the facts.

And yet the reality of ineffable meaning is, as we have shown, beyond dispute. The imperative of awe is its certificate of evidence, a universal certificate which we all witness and seal with tremor and spasm, *not* because we desire to, but because we are stunned and cannot brave it. There is so much more meaning in reality than my soul can take in! And when I begin to spell the infinite sentence of my amazement and to say what I perceive, I realize that all perception is an externalization, that the essence begins where perception ends. The perception of its surpassing my power of perception is too consistent, staggering and universal to be illusory.

The ultimate question, therefore, is not the mind's *creatio ex nihilo* but a reiteration in the mind of what is given to the soul. The indication of what transcends all things is given to us with the same immediacy as the things themselves. Its presence is as much a fact as any other; it is, indeed, much more—it is a fact within all facts. For while it is true that the conceivable aspects of reality are next to our experience; within experience it is the mystery upon which we come. While our minds are upon things, our souls are carried away beyond them.

A SPIRITUAL PRESENCE

Awareness of a mystery is shared by all men. Yet, as we have seen, they usually mistake what they sense as being apart from their own existence, as if there were only wonder in what they see, not in the very act of seeing, as if the mystery were merely an object of observation. Unsparing, unqualified thinking opens our minds to the fact, that the mystery is not apart from ourselves, not a far-off thing like a rainbow in the sky; the mystery is out of doors, in all things to be seen, not only where there is more than what the senses can grasp. Those to whom awareness of the ineffable is a constant state of mind know that the mystery is not an exception but an air that lies about all being, a spiritual setting of reality; not something apart but a *dimension* of all existence.

They learn to sense that all existence is embraced by a *spiritual presence*; that life is not a property of the self; that the world is an open house in which the presence of the owner is so well concealed that we usually mistake His discretion for nonexistence.

There is a holiness that hovers over all things, that makes them look to us in some moments like objects of transcendent meditation, as if *to be* meant *to be thought of* by God,* as if all external life were embraced by an inner life, by a process within a mind, pensive, intentional. Numbers, abstract relations, express its essence as little as the number of the members of a family tell the unique story of their drama. (Inner life, being thought of, is, of course, a simile, but it is only in similes that we can communicate when speaking of the ultimate.)

To the religious man it is as if things stood with *their back to him, their faces turned to God*, as if the ineffable quality of things consisted in their being an object of divine thought. Just as in touching a tree we know that the tree is not the end

* See p. 128.

64

of the world, that the tree stands in space, so we know that the ineffable—what is holy in justice, compassion and truthfulness—is not the end of spirit; that the ultimate values survive our misjudgments, deflations and repudiations; that meaning is meaningful not because of our minds; that beauty is beautiful not by the grace of man.

The soul is introduced to a reality which is not only *other* than itself, as it is the case in the ordinary acts of perception; it is introduced to a reality which is *higher* than the universe. Our soul compares with its glory as a breath with all the world's air. We are introduced to a reality, the mere awareness of which is more precious to us than our own existence. The thought of it is too powerful to be ignored and too holy to be absorbed by us. It is a thought in which we share. It is as if the human mind were not alone in thinking it, but the whole universe were full of it. We do not wonder *at* things any more; we wonder *with* all things. We do not think about things; we think for all things.

9 In the Presence of God

The sense of the ineffable introduces the soul to the divine aspect of the universe, to a reality higher than the universe. However, in stating that to be means to be thought of by God, that the universe is an object of divine thought, we have affirmed the existence of a being who is beyond the ineffable. How do we know that God is more than the holy dimension, more than an aspect or an attribute of being? How do we go from the allusiveness of the world—to a being to whom the world alludes?

In thinking on the level of the ineffable, we do not set out with a preconceived idea of a supreme being in our possession, trying to ascertain whether He is in reality the way He is in our minds. The awareness which opens our minds to the existence of a supreme being is an awareness of reality, an awareness of a divine presence. Long before we attain any knowledge about His *essence*, we possess an intuition of a divine *presence*.

This is wherein the approach through the ineffable differs from the approach through speculation. In the latter we proceed from an idea of His essence to a belief in His existence, while in the former we proceed from an intuition of His presence to an understanding of His essence.

The sense of the ineffable does not give us an awareness of God. It only leads to a plane, where no one can remain both callous and calm, unstunned and unabashed; where His presence may be defied but not denied, and where, at the end, faith in Him is the only way.

Once our bare soul is exposed to the omnipresence of the ineffable, we cannot bid it cease to shatter us with its urging wonder. It is as if there were only signs and hidden reminders of the one and only true subject, of whom the world is a cryptic object.

Who lit the wonder before our eyes and the wonder of our eyes? Who struck the lightning in the minds and scorched us with an imperative of being overawed by the holy as unquenchable as the sight of the stars?

The beginning of faith is not a feeling for the mystery of living or a sense of awe, wonder or fear. The root of religion is the question what to do with the feeling for the mystery of living, what to do with awe, wonder or fear. Religion, the end of isolation, begins with a consciousness that something is asked of us. It is in that tense, eternal asking in which the soul is caught and in which man's answer is elicited.

Wonder is not a state of esthetic enjoyment. Endless wonder is endless tension, a situation in which we are shocked at the inadequacy of our awe, at the weakness of our shock, as well as the state of being asked the ultimate question.

Endless wonder unlocks an innate sense of indebtedness. Within our awe there is no place for self-assertion. Within our awe we only know that all we own we owe. The world consists, not of things, but of tasks. Wonder is the state of our being asked. The ineffable is a question addressed to us.

All that is left to us is a choice—to answer or to refuse to answer. Yet the more deeply we listen, the more we become stripped of the arrogance and callousness which alone would enable us to refuse. We carry a load of marvel, wishing to exchange it for the simplicity of knowing what to live for, a load which we can never lay down nor continue to carry not knowing where.

At the moment in which a fire bursts forth, threatening to destroy one's home, a person does not pause to investigate whether the danger he faces is real or a figment of his imagination. Such a moment is not the time to inquire into the chemical principle of combustion, or into the question of who is to blame for the outbreak of the fire. The ultimate question, when bursting forth in our souls, is too startling, too heavily laden with unutterable wonder to be an academic question, to be equally suspended between yes and no. Such a moment is not the time to throw doubts upon the reason for the rise of the question.

69

When we think with all our mind, with all our heart, with all our soul; when we become aware of the fact that the self cannot stand on its own, we realize that the most subtle explanations are splendid enigmas, that God is more plausible than our own selves, that it is not God who is an enigma but we. When all our mind is aglow with the eternal question like a face in gazing on a mighty blaze, we are not moved to ask: Where is God? for such a question would imply that we who ask are present, while God is absent. In the realm of the ineffable, where our own presence is incredible, we do not ask: Where is God? We can only exclaim: Where is He not? Where are we? How is our presence possible?

At the moment in which we are stirred for the first time by the ultimate question we unreservedly confess our inability to face the world without a being which is beyond the world. Our question is in essence a foregone conclusion, an answer in disguise. For once we accept the legitimacy of the question, we have affirmed it. Failure of our mind to find evidence for His presence is merely an implied admission that we consider nature to be so perfect that no trace of its being dependent upon the supernatural can be detected; it is as if God had poured out a splendor to conceal His presence.

Yet there is a dimension where God is not concealed, wherein we sense His presence behind the splendor. But are we able to say what we sense? Are we able to lay bare the inmost reason for our certainty of the existence of a being who surpasses all glory?

70

Man is not alone

The issue that emerges before us is not whether there is a God, but whether we know that there is a God; not whether He exists, but whether we are intelligent enough to advance adequate reasons for affirming it. The problem is: How do we tell it to our minds? How do we overcome the antinomies that bar us from knowing clearly and distinctly what He means?

THE INVINCIBLE QUESTION

Awareness of the divine that intrudes first as a sense of wonder gleaming through indifference, as a compulsion to be aware of the ineffable, grows, imperceptibly, like a hair, to uneasiness, anxiety, until it bristles with an unbearable concern that deprives us of complacency and peace of mind, forcing us to care for ends which we do not wish to care for, for ends which have no appeal to our personal interest. With all our might, pride and self-reliance, we try to defy, to suppress and to combat that concern for the unregarded, for that which is unconfined by either mind or will or our own life. We would rather be prisoners, if only our mind, will, passion and ambitions were the four walls of the prison. There would, indeed, be no greater comfort than to live in the security of foregone conclusions, if not for that gnawing concern which turns all conclusions into a shambles.

What is the nature of that enforced concern we resist so vehemently? It is not our own; it is a pressure that weighs upon us as well as upon all men. It does not impart any words; it only asks, it only calls. It plants a question, a behest, in front of us, which our heart echoes like a bell, overpowering as if it were the only sound in endless stillness and we the only ones to answer it. Our mind, our voice is too coarse to utter a reply. It is a question that demands our whole being as an answer. Our words, possessions, achievements are no longer an answer. Theories, explanations dissipate as mere diversions. We cease to see the answers for the question, the trees for the forest. There are neither skies nor oceans, neither birds nor trees—there is only a question, and the question is ineffable.

IN SEARCH OF A SOUL

Pursued by a question we are unable to fathom, one which does not fit in our intellectual curiosity, we are caught in its struggle to find a way to our minds, in its quest of a soul to engage itself in its understanding.

We cannot question the supreme invincible question that extends in front of us, opening itself to us like time, unremittingly, and pleading with us like a voice that had been melted into stillness.

There is no knowledge that would be an answer to endless wonder, that could stem the tide of its silent challenge. When we are overtaken by endless wonder, all inference is an awkward retrogression; in such moments a syllogism is not self-evident but an insight is. In such moments our logical affirmation, our saying yes, appears like a bubble of thought at the strand of an eternal sea. We, then, realize that our concern is not: What may we know? How could we open Him to our minds? Our concern is: To whom do we belong? How could we open our lives to Him?

Where self-assertion is no more; when realizing that wonder is not our own achievement; that it is not by our own power alone that we are shuddered with radical amazement, it is not within our power any more to assume the role of an examiner of a subject in search of an object, such as we are in search of a cause when perceiving thunder. Ultimate wonder is not the same as curiosity. Curiosity is the state of a mind in search of knowledge, while ultimate wonder is the state of knowledge in search of a mind; it is the thought of God in search of a soul.

What is decisive is not the existential moment of despair, the acceptance of our own bankruptcy, but, on the contrary, the realization of our great spiritual power, the power to heal what is broken in the world, the realization of our capacity to answer God's question.

Faith is not a product of our will. It occurs without intention, without will. Words expire when uttered, and faith is like the silence that draws lovers near, like a breath that shares in the wind.

It is neither an inference from logical premises nor the outcome of a feeling that leads us to believe in His existence; it is not an idea gained by sitting back and observing or by going into the soul and listening to one's inner voice. We do not believe because we have come to a conclusion . . . or because we have been overcome by an emotion. . . . It is a turning within the mind by a power from beyond the mind, a shock and collision with the unbelievable by which we are coerced into believing.

Speculative proof is no prelude to faith. The antecedents of faith are the premise of the wonder and the premise of praise. We praise before we prove. While in regard to other issues we doubt before we decide, in regard to God we sing before we say. Unless we know how to praise Him, we cannot learn how to know Him. Praise is our first answer to the wonder. Indeed, in the face of the sublime what is left for us to do except to praise, to be aflame with the inability to say what we see and to feel ashamed of not knowing how to thank for the ability to see?

To be overtaken with awe of God is not to entertain a feeling but to share in a spirit that permeates all beings. "They all thank, they all praise, they all say: There is no one like God." As an act of personal recognition our praise would be fatuous, it is only meaningful as an act of joining in the endless song. We praise with the pebbles on the road which are like petrified amazement, with all the flowers and trees which look as if hypnotized in silent devotion.

When mind and soul agree, belief is born. But first our hearts must know the shudder of adoration.

LET THE INSIGHT BE

Our awareness of God is a syntax of the silence, in which our souls mingle with the divine, in which the ineffable in us com-

74

munes with the ineffable beyond us. It is the afterglow of years in which soul and sky are silent together, the outgrowth of accumulated certainty of the abundant, never-ebbing presence of the divine. All we ought to do is to let the insight be and to listen to the soul's recessed certainty of its being a parenthesis in the immense script of God's eternal speech.

The great insight is not attained when we ponder or infer the beyond from the here. In the realm of the ineffable, God is not a hypothesis derived from logical assumptions, but an immediate insight, self-evident as light. He is not something to be sought in the darkness with the light of reason. In the face of the ineffable He *is* the light. When the ultimate awareness comes, it is like a flash, arriving all at once. To meditative minds the ineffable is cryptic, inarticulate: dots, marks of secret meaning, scattered hints, to be gathered, deciphered and formed into evidence; while in moments of insight the ineffable is a metaphor in a forgotten mother tongue.

Thus, awareness of God does not come by degrees: from timidity to intellectual temerity; from guesswork, reluctance, to certainty; it is not a decision reached at the crossroads of doubt. It comes when, drifting in the wilderness, having gone astray, we suddenly behold the immutable polar star. Out of endless anxiety, out of denial and despair, the soul bursts out in speechless crying.

GOD IS SUING FOR MAN

To knock timidly at distant gates of silence, inquiring whether there is a God somewhere, is not the way. We all have the power to discover in the nearest stone or tree, sound or thought, the shelter of His often desecrated goodness, His waiting for man's heart to affiliate with His will. It is a travail to perceive the unfolding of the divine in this world of strife and envy. Yet a force from beyond our conscience cries at man, reminding and admonishing that the wanton will fail in rebellion against the good. He who is willing to be an echo to that pleading voice opens his life to the comprehension of the unseen in the desert of indifference. It is God who sues for our devotion, constantly, persistently, who goes out to meet us as soon as we long to know Him.

What gives birth to religion is not intellectual curiosity, but the fact and experience of our being asked. As long as we frame and ponder our own questions, we do not even know how to ask. We know too little to be able to inquire. Faith is not the product of search and endeavor, but the answer to a challenge which no one can forever ignore. It is ushered in not by a problem, but by an exclamation. Philosophy begins with man's question; *religion begins with God's question and man's answer.*

He who chooses a life of utmost striving for the utmost stake, the vital, matchless stake of God, feels at times as though the spirit of God rested upon his eyelids—close to his eyes and yet never seen. He who has realized that sun and stars and souls do not ramble in a vacuum will keep his heart in readiness for the hour when the world is entranced. For things are not mute: the stillness is full of demands, awaiting a soul to breathe in the mystery that all things exhale in their craving for communion. Out of the world comes a behest to instill into the air a rapturous song for God, to incarnate in stones a message of humble beauty, and to instill a prayer for goodness in the hearts of all men.

THE ENFORCED CONCERN

The world in which we live is a vast cage within a maze, high as our mind, wide as our power of will, long as our life span. Those who have never reached the rails or seen what is beyond the cage know of no freedom to dream of and are willing to rise and fight for civilizations that come and go and sink into the abyss of oblivion, an abyss which they never fill.

In our technological age man could not conceive of this world as anything but material for his own fulfilment. He considered himself the sovereign of his destiny, capable of organizing the breeding of races, of adapting a philosophy to his transient needs and of creating a religion at will. He postulated the existence of a Power that would serve as a guarantee for his self-fulfilment, as if God were a henchman to cater to man's aspirations and help him draw the utmost out of life.

But even those who have knocked their heads against the rails of the cage and discovered that life is involved in conflicts which they cannot solve; that the drive of possessiveness, which fills streets, homes and hearts with its clamor and shrill, is constantly muffled by the irony of time; that our constructiveness is staved in by self-destructiveness—even they prefer to live on the sumptuous, dainty diet within the cage rather than look for an exit to the maze in order to search for freedom in the darkness of the undisclosed.

Others, however, who cannot stand it, despair. They have

no power to spend on faith any more, no goal to strive for, no strength to seek a goal. But, then, a moment comes like a thunderbolt, in which a flash of the undisclosed rends our dark apathy asunder. It is full of overpowering brilliance, like a point in which all moments of life are focused or a thought which outweighs all thoughts ever conceived of. There is so much light in our cage, in our world, it is as if it were suspended amidst the stars. Apathy turns to splendor unawares. The ineffable has shuddered itself into the soul. It has entered our consciousness like a ray of light passing into a lake. Refraction of that penetrating ray brings about a turning in our mind: We are penetrated by His insight. We cannot think any more as if He were there and we here. He is both there and here. He is not *a being*, but *being in and beyond all beings.*

A tremor seizes our limbs; our nerves are struck, quiver like strings; our whole being bursts into shudders. But then a cry, wrested from our very core, fills the world around us, as if a mountain were suddenly about to place itself in front of us. It is one word: GOD. Not an emotion, a stir within us, but a power, a marvel beyond us, tearing the world apart. The word that means more than universe, more than eternity, holy, holy, holy; we cannot comprehend it. We only know it means infinitely more than we are able to echo. Staggered, embarrassed, we stammer and say: He, who is more than all there is, who speaks through the ineffable, whose question is more than our mind can answer; He to whom our life can be the spelling of an answer.

An inspiration passes, having been inspired never passes. It remains like an island across the restlessness of time, to which we move over the wake of undying wonder. An eagerness is left behind, a craving and a feeling of shame at our ever being tainted with oblivion . . .

We may be able to say no, if we decide to feed our mind on presumption and conceit, to cling to duplicity and to refuse to mean what we sense, to think what we feel. But there is no man who is not shaken for an instant by the eternal. And if we claim we have no heart to feel, no soul to hear, let us pray for tears or a feeling of shame.

10 Doubts

Afterwards, when man's sense of the ineffable is at its ebb and the coercion of invasive insights is vanishing, the eternal question appears to be out of tune in the din of acquisitiveness and commonplace thinking. The mind in its honesty tolls its doubts. Is the encounter with the ineffable, in which one learns about the existence of a being beyond the ineffable, to be considered a reliable source of insight? That encounter may be nothing but a soliloquy, the insight acquired therein a figment of the mind, an outgrowth of the will.

There are, indeed, no credentials in our possession by which we could demonstrate to others that the endless concern in which we were initiated is not the outpouring of our own heart. Even responsiveness to the ineffable cannot be demonstrated, how much less can we kindle that to which we respond, as if to set the bush afire with God for all men to see.

No one can be a witness to the nonexistence of God without laying perjury upon his soul, for those who abscond, those who are always absent when God is present, have only the right to establish their alibi for their not being able to bear witness.

The ultimate question in its logical form is an ever-present challenge which we encounter wherever we turn, and there is no way of ignoring it. Man cannot afford to be noncommittal about a reality upon which the meaning and manner of his existence depend. He is driven toward some sort of affirmation. In whatever decision he makes, he implicitly accepts either the presence of God or the absurdity of denying it. The nonsense of denial is too monstrous to be conceivable, since it implies that the universe is all alone except for the company of man, that the mind of man surpasses everything within and beyond the universe. Unless we forget what happens to us in the unimpaired state of sensing the ineffable, in our speechless amazement, when most of our concepts are discarded as self-mindedness and conceits are on the wane, we cannot maintain that man has the monopoly of mind and soul, that he is the only being alive and conscious within and beyond the universe, that there is no spirit except the spirit of man. Those who are open to the ineffable will beware of spiritual schizophrenia; namely, the loss of contact with the mystery of living that surrounds us everywhere and at all times. On the other hand, he who affirms the existence of God, though he may not be able to defend the epistemological consistency of his judgment, remains consistent with his living awareness of the ineffable.

The sense of the ineffable is earlier and stronger than doubts. Logical proofs for the existence of God come as an anticlimax to those who have been set astir by that which concepts are trying to ascertain.

In trying to prove or disprove the existence of God, we are like dancing puppets which, incapable of knowing for what end and how they are capable of dancing, presume to judge about whether or not anyone is pulling the strings. Those who find it impossible to subsist on the rational diet of the rational soul will not be able to perform the solemn ceremony of extending *de jure* recognition to God after His existence has been conclusively demonstrated and duly confirmed.

When the soul is not aflame, no light of speculation will illumine the darkness of indifference. No masterly logical demonstration of God's existence or any analysis of the intricacies of the traditional God-concepts will succeeed in dispersing that darkness. Men have almost unlearned the art of being convinced by means of abstractions about ultimate reality, and the austere dignity of abstract logical evidence seldom prevails over the misgivings of intellectual inertia. It is naïve to assume that it was because of Kant's refutation of the classical proofs for the existence of God that modern man has forfeited his faith. His faith was lost long before his skepticism began.

Proofs may aid in protecting, but not in initiating certainty; essentially they are explications of what is already intuitively clear to us.

He who seeks God to suit his doubts, to appease his skepticism or to satisfy his curiosity, fails to find the whereabouts of the issue. Search for God begins with the realization that it is man who is the problem; that more than God is a problem to man, man is a problem to Him.

If the divine were a complex notion, then we might have suspected it to be a product of fancy, a combination of characteristics found separately in the world and which are imagined to exist together in one being. But the divine as a first insight is a reality, transcending both the power of mind and the order of the world rather than a compound of characteristics found within the world.

The divine is too ineffable to be a product of the human

mind, too grave, demanding and all-surpassing to be postulated by wishful thinking. Where would such an awareness of the all-surpassing being come from, if not from an underivable insight into His all-surpassingness? The question, however, may be asked: Don't we often cherish beliefs which are afterwards exposed as delusions? Yes: we may believe that we see a house when driving through the desert and upon trying to reach it, it may turn out to be a mirage. But we cannot think that a picture represents a house if there is no such thing as a house.*

The most basic objection to the belief in the existence of God is the argument that such a belief passes from the mind's data to something that surpasses the scope of the mind. What gives us the assurance that an idea which we may find ourselves obliged to think may hold true of a reality that lies beyond the reach of the mind? Such an objection is valid when applied to the speculative approach. Yet, as we have seen, the certainty of the existence of God does not come about as a corollary of logical premises, as a leap from the realm of logic to the realm of ontology, from an assumption to a fact. It is, on the contrary, a transition from an immediate apprehension to a thought, from being overwhelmed by the presence of God to an awareness of His essence.

In sensing the spiritual dimension of all being, we become aware of the absolute reality of the divine. In formulating a creed, in asserting: God exists, we merely bring down overpowering reality to the level of thought. Our belief is but an afterthought.

In other words, our belief in the reality of God is not a case of first possessing an idea and then postulating the ontal

* Compare *Collected Papers* of Ch. S. Peirce, 6. 493.

counterpart to it; or, to use a Kantian phrase, of first having the idea of a hundred dollars and then claiming to possess them on the basis of the idea. What obtains here is first the actual possession of the dollars and then the attempt to count the sum. There are possibilities of error in counting the notes, but the notes themselves are here.

The decisive phase, the transition from obliviousness to an awareness of God, is not a leap over a missing link in a syllogism but a retreat, giving up premises rather than adding one, going behind self-consciousness and questioning the self and all its cognitive pretensions.

We have no power to reach the climax of thought, no wings upon which to rise and to leave all dangers of distortion behind. But we are at times ablaze against and beyond our own power, and unless human existence is dismissed as an insane asylum, the spectrum analysis of that ray is evidence for those who look for it.

11 Faith

Men have often tried to give itemized accounts of why they must believe that God exists. Such accounts are like ripe wheat we harvest upon the surface of the earth. Yet it is beyond all reasons, beneath the ground, where a seed turns to be a tree, where the act of faith takes place.

The soul rarely knows how to raise its deeper secrets to discursive levels of the mind. We must not, therefore, equate the act of faith with its expression. The expression of faith is an affirmation of truth, a definite judgment, a conviction, while faith itself is an act, something that happens rather than something that is stored away; it is a moment in which the soul of man communes with the glory of God.

What is the nature of that act? How does it come about?

The question of the psalmist: "Is there a man of reason who seeks God?" (14:2), was interpreted by Rabbi Mendel of Kotzk to mean: Is a man who has nothing but his own reason capable of seeking God?

Many of us are willing to embark upon any adventure, except to go into stillness and to wait, to place all the wealth of wisdom in the secrecy of the soil, to sow our own soul for a seed in that tract of land allocated to every life which we call time—and to let the soul grow beyond itself. Faith is the fruit of a seed planted in the depth of a lifetime.

Many of us seem to think that faith is a convenient short cut to the mystery of God across the endless, dizzy highway of critical speculation. The truth is that faith is not a way but the breaking of a way, of the soul's passageway constantly to be dug through mountains of callousness. Faith is neither a gift which we receive undeservedly nor a treasure to be found inadvertently.

We do not stumble into achievements. Faith is the fruit of hard, constant care and vigilance, of insistence upon remaining true to a vision; not an act of inertia but an aspiration to maintain our responsiveness to Him alive.

Just as men are unable to notice the most obvious phenomena in nature unless they are anxious to know about them—as no scientific insight will occur to those who are unprepared—so are they incapable of grasping the divine unless they grow sensitive to its supreme relevance. Without cleanliness of will the mind is impervious to the relevance of God.

To a savage who appreciates only the commodities of his tribe a violin may appear to be a queer piece of wood. Indeed, there are always people to whom all songs, all melodies sound alike.

The art of awareness of God, the art of sensing His presence in our daily lives cannot be learned off-hand. God's grace resounds in our lives like a staccato. Only by retaining the seemingly disconnected notes comes the ability to grasp the theme.

Man is not alone

Faith will come to him who passionately yearns for ultimate meaning, who is alert to the sublime dignity of being, who is alive to the marvel of matter, to the unbelievable core within the known, evident, concrete.

In order to grasp what is so overwhelmingly obvious to the pious man, we must suspend the trivialities of thinking that stultify unique insights and decline to stifle our minds with standardized notions. The greatest obstacle to faith is the inclination to be content with half-truths and half-realities. Faith is only given to him who lives with all his mind and all his soul; who strives for understanding with all beings not only for knowledge about them; whose permanent concern is the cultivation of our *uncommon* sense, education in sensing the ineffable.* Faith is found in solicitude for faith, in a passionate care for the marvel that is everywhere.

Highest in the list of virtues, this partisan care extends not only to the moral sphere but to all realms of life: to oneself and to others, to words and to thoughts, to events and to deeds. Unawed by the prevailing narrowness of mind, it persists as an attitude toward the whole of reality: to hold small things great, to take light matters seriously, to think of daily

* "For the nature of the self-evident is not to be evident to every mind however undeveloped, but to be apprehended directly by minds which have reached a certain degree of maturity, and for minds to reach the necessary degree of maturity the development that takes place from generation to generation is as much needed as that which takes place from infancy to adult life." W. D. Ross, *The Right and the Good*, p. 12.

89

affairs in relation to the everlasting. It is not an attitude of detachment from reality, of passive absorption or of self-annihilation, but rather the ability to witness the holy within this world's affairs, and to entertain a feeling of shame and discontent with living without faith, without responsiveness to the holy.

Strange and scattered are the wells from which we draw the transport of such discontent. Some of us are sickened by the dismay of living constantly for naught, by the dread of an unprepared death; some are distressed by the way in which the innocence of our own limbs and words is exposed to our rude and reckless power. Others are charmed by the sanctity of living for His laws. Instead of indulging in jealousy and greed, instead of relishing themselves, they decide to keep their hearts alert to the allusiveness which surrounds us everywhere.

By foregoing beauty for goodness, power for love, grief for gratitude, by entreating the Lord for help to understand our hopes, for strength to resist our fears, we may receive a gentle sense of the holiness permeating the air like a strangeness that cannot be removed. Our crying out of pitfalls of self-indulgence for purity of devotion will prepare the dawn of faith.

Some men go on a hunger strike in the prison of the mind, starving for God. There is joy, ancient and sudden, in this starving. There is reward, a grasp of the intangible, in the flaming reverie breaking through the bars of thought.

Man is not alone

SOME OF US BLUSH

God is unwilling to be alone, and man cannot forever re-main impervious to what He longs to show. Those of us who cannot keep their striving back find themselves at times within the sight of the unseen and become aglow with its rays Some of us blush, others wear a mask. Faith is a blush in the presence of God.

Some of us blush, others wear a mask which veils spontane-ous sensivity to the holy ineffable dimension of reality. We all wear so much mental make-up, we have almost forfeited our face. But faith only comes when we stand face to face— the ineffable in us with the ineffable beyond us—suffer our-selves to be seen, to commune, to receive a ray and to reflect it. But to do that the soul must be alive within the mind.

Responsiveness to God cannot be copied; it must be orig-inal with every soul. Even the meaning of the divine is not grasped when imposed by a doctrine, when accepted by hear-say. It only enters our vision when leaping like a spark from the anvil of the mind, hammered and beaten upon by trem-bling awe.

Those who search after Him in abstractions will miss Him. He is not a lost pearl at the bottom of the mind, to be found when diving in the waves of argument. The greatest is never that which you expect.

It is in our inability to grasp Him that we come closest to Him. The existence of God is not real because it is conceiv-able; it is conceivable because it is real. And real it is to him who learns to live in tremor and awe for no purpose, for no reward; who abides in tremor and awe because he could not do otherwise; who lives in the awareness of the ineffable, even though it may seem foolish, futile and improper.

Thinking about God as a hobby, as a part-time occupation, will fail even to set forth the issue. For what is the issue in which we are involved? Is it curiosity of the kind we entertain when being inquisitive about the nature of electronics? Electronics does not ask anything of us, while the beginning of what God means is the awareness of our being committed to Him.

God is not an explanation of the world's enigmas or a guarantee for our salvation. He is an eternal challenge, an urgent demand. He is not a problem to be solved but a question addressed to us as individuals, as nations, as mankind.

God is of no importance unless He is of supreme importance, which means a deep certainty that it is better to be defeated with Him than be victorious without Him.

THE TEST OF FAITH

The man who lives by his faith is he who—even if scholars the world over should proclaim, if all mankind by an overwhelming majority of votes should endorse and if experiments, which at times adapt themselves to man's favorite theories, should corroborate that there is no God—would rather suffer at the hands of reason than accept his own reason as an idol; who would grieve, but neither totter nor betray the dignity of his sense of inadequacy in the presence of the ineffable. For faith is an earnest we hold till the hour of pass-

92

ing away, not to be redeemed by a doctrine or even exchanged for insights. What God means is expressed in the words: "For Thy kindness is better than life" (Psalms 63:4). God is He whose regard for me I value more than life.

Faith is not captured in observing events in the physical world that deviate from the known laws of nature. Of what avail are miracles, with our senses unreliable, with our knowledge incomplete? Faith precedes any palpable experience, rather than derives from it. Without possessing faith, no experience will communicate to us religious significance.

It says in The Song of Songs: "As an apple-tree among the trees of the wood" (2:3). Rabbi Aha ben Zeira made a comparison: "The apple-tree brings out its blossom before its leaves, so Israel in Egypt had achieved faith even before they perceived the message of redemption, as it says: 'And the people believed; and they heard that the Lord had remembered' (Exodus 4; 31)" (Midrash Hazita 2, 10).

A saying of Rabbi Isaac Meir of Ger may illustrate what we mean. Commenting on the verse: "And Israel saw the great work which the Lord did upon the Egyptians, and the people feared the Lord; and they had faith in the Lord, and in His servant Moses" (Exodus 14:31), he remarked: "Although they saw the miracles with their own eyes, they were still in need of faith, because faith is superior to sight; with faith you see more than with your eyes."

AN ACT OF SPIRIT

In the light of faith we do not seek to unveil or to explain but to perceive and to absorb the rarities of mystery that shine out from all things; not to know more but to be attached to what is more than anything we can grasp. Only those who maintain that all things in life and death are within reach of their will, try to place the world within the frame of their knowledge. But who can forever remain insensitive to the fragrance of the holy bestowed upon life?

With the gentle sense for the divine in all existence, for the sacred relevance of all being, the pious man can afford to forego the joy of knowing, the thrill of perceiving. He who loves the grandeur of what faith discloses dwells at a distance from his goal, eschews familiarity with what is necessarily hidden and looks for neither proofs nor miracles. God's existence can never be tested by human thought. All proofs are mere demonstrations of our thirst for Him. Does the thirsty one need proof of his thirst?

The realm toward which faith is directed can be approached but not penetrated; approximated but not entered; aspired to but not grasped; sensed but not examined. For to have faith is to abide rationally outside, while spiritually within, the mystery.

Faith is an act of the spirit. The spirit can afford to acknowledge the superiority of the divine; it has the fortitude to realize the greatness of the transcendent, to love its superiority. The man of faith is not enticed by the ostensible. He abstains from intellectual arrogance and spurns the triumph of the merely obvious. He knows that possession of truth is devotion to it. Rejoicing more in giving than in acquiring, more in believing than in perceiving, he can afford to disregard the deficiencies of reason. This is the secret of the spirit, not disclosed to reason: the adaptation of the mind to what is sacred, intellectual humility in the presence of the supreme. The mind surrenders to the mystery of spirit, not in resignation but in love. Exposing its destiny to the ultimate, it enters into an intimate relationship with God.

Is it surrender to confide? Is it a sacrifice to believe? True, beliefs are not secured by demonstration nor are they impregnable to objection. But does goodness mean serving only as long as rewarding lasts? Towers are more apt to be shaken than graves. Insistent doubt, contest and frustration may stultify the trustworthy mind, may turn temples into shambles. Those of faith who plant sacred thoughts in the uplands of time—the secret gardeners of the Lord in mankind's desolate hopes—may slacken and tarry, but they rarely betray their vocation.

It is extremely easy to be cynical. It is as easy to deny His existence as it is to commit suicide. Yet no one is deprived of some measure of *suggestibility to the Holy*. Even the poorest souls have wings, soaring above where despair sees a ceiling.

12 What Do We Mean By the Divine?

The great secret seems to have no affinity with tenets of any kind. There is hardly a symbol which, when used, would not impair or even undo the grasp or remembrance of the incomparable. Opinions confuse and stand in the way of intuitions; surveys, definitions take the name of God in vain. We have neither an image nor a definition of God. We have only His name. And the name is ineffable.

The pious man, therefore, is not distinguished by passion for uttering in words what he knows, conscious of the danger of expending the best beyond recall. In expressing, one is delivered of what he is replete with, and the pious man's desire is to live it rather than to be released of it. Eloquence is a gift rarely given to saints. It is natural, too, that the utterance of the most profound is tridimensional, its literal meaning reflecting merely the surface of that which the utterance is trying to convey.

If a poet and a pious man should confer and exchange views, the poet would say: "All he lives, I say"; and the pious man would know: "All he says, I live."

It is the theoretician, who, rather than standing face to face with the mystery, holds his mental mirrors against it, making myths of mysteries, computing dogmas of enigmas and worshipping the image in the mirrors. He does not seem to realize that idolization of ideas leads to an atrophy of the intuition of the ineffable; that God may be lost in our creed, in our worship, in our dogmas.

To say how our thoughts detect the patina of the holy on the surface of the common is worth spending a lifetime. But thoughts in which such detection can be told are scarce, and the most vital words die when spoken. This is why God begins where words end.

Yet no one can live on mystery alone. The awareness of the ineffable is like listening to a question, to a behest. Something is asked of us. But what? We are driven to know God in order to conform to His ways. But to know Him we would have to attain the nearly impossible: to render the ineffable in positive terms. The question, then, arises: If, in order to be known, the ineffable has to be expressed, does it not follow that we know it as it is not?

Religious insights have to be carried over a long distance to reach expression, and they may easily shrivel or even perish on the way from the heart to the lips. Our awareness is immediate, but our interpretations are discursive. They are often casualties of the soul's congested traffic, particularly when under the strain of realizing more than the heart can hear, we compromise with words that carry us away.

The intuition of God is universal, yet there is hardly a universal form—with few possible exceptions—to express it. Indeed, the conceptions of the divine have differed widely and contradicted each other, often flourishing like noisome weeds, inflicting sting and discord. If uniformity and impeccability of expression were the mark of authenticity, such divergence and distortion would refute our assumption of the reality of the mystery. The fact, however, is that men's opinions about God throughout history do not show a greater variety than, for example, their opinions about the nature of the world.

STANDARDS OF EXPRESSION

We must beware lest we violate the holy, lest our dogmas overthink the mystery, lest our psalms sing it away. The right of interpretation is given only to one who covers his face, "afraid to look at God," to one who, when the vision is forced upon him, says: "I am undone . . . for mine eyes have seen the King." We can only drink the flow of thoughts out of the rock of their words. Only words that would not be trite in the presence of a dying man, only ideas that would not pale in the face of the rising sun or in the midst of a violent earthquake: "God is One" or: "Holy, Holy, Holy is the Lord of Hosts . . ." may be used as metaphors in speaking of God.

The ineffable will only enter a word in the way in which the hour to come will enter the path of time: when there shall be no other hours in the way. It will speak when of all words only one will be worthwhile. For the mystery is not always evasive. It confides itself at rare moments to those who are chosen. We cannot express God, yet God expresses His will to us. It is through His word that we know that God is not beyond good and evil. Our emotion would leave us in a state of bewilderment, if not for the guidance we received.

How do we identify the divine? In order to recognize what it is, we would have to know it. But if our knowledge were contingent upon acts of a divine communication, we might never be able to identify such a communication as divine.

Moreover, an idea does not become valid or credible by virtue of the circumstances in which it enters our mind. We cannot plead truth in the name of the throes under which it was born. Any message that claims to be divine must stand on its own and be saturated with a unique meaningfulness which would identify it as divine. If a person should appear among us and proclaim an idea communicated to him in a miraculous manner, and our critical examinations should even confirm the miraculous manner of his experience, would we for that matter feel obliged to accept his idea as valid and true?

Nor should our own inner experiences fare better. We must be in possession of an *a priori* idea of the divine, of a quality or relation representing to us the ultimate, by which we would be able to identify it when given to us in such acts.

Compellingness is not a mark of the highest nor is our feeling or being in a state of absolute dependence an index of His presence. Physical force or inner obsessions may overpower us with irresistible compellingness and, as has often been pointed out, a survivor of a wrecked ship embracing a floating board is in a state of absolute dependence upon the board.

No inquiry can get under way without some presupposition or perspective to start from. The scientist in formulating a problem must anticipate, in some measure, the content of the solution he is aiming at, for otherwise he would neither know what he asks about nor be able to judge whether the solutions he will find will be relevant to his problem. Philosophy has been defined as a science with a minimum of presuppositions, for there is no way of proceeding in our thoughts without any perspective, without any initial assumption.

Such an initial assumption lies at the beginning of all speculation about God. To the speculative mind God is the most perfect being, and it is the attribute of perfection and its implication of wisdom which serve as a starting point for the inquiries into the existence and nature of God.

THE ATTRIBUTE OF PERFECTION

The notion of God as a perfect being is not of biblical extraction. It is the product not of prophetic religion but of Greek philosophy; a postulate of reason rather than a direct, compelling, initial answer of man to His reality. In the Decalogue, God does not speak of His being perfect but of His having made free men out of slaves. Signifying a state of being without defect and lack, perfection is a term of praise which we may utter in pouring forth our emotion; yet for man to utter it as a name for His essence would mean to evaluate and to endorse Him. The biblical language is free of such insolence, it only dared to call "His work" (Deuteronomy 32:4), "His way" (II Samuel 22:31) or the "Torah" (Psalm 19:7) *tamim*, perfect.

101

We were never told: "Hear, O Israel, God is perfect!" It is an attribution which is strikingly absent in both the biblical and rabbinic literature.

Who are we to appraise Him or even to name Him? We never pronounce the Ineffable Name and utter instead a paraphrase—the Lord—which, in our vocabulary, is a title of minor distinction. This, according to Rabbi Pinchas of Koretz, is not due to the fact that His majesty is limited, but because our world is of minor importance. A great emperor holds among his many appellations the title "sovereign" of a certain island. That title is of minor worth, because the island is small in size.*

There is, however, one idea that carries our thoughts beyond the horizon of our island; an idea which addresses itself to all minds and is tacitly accepted as an axiom by science and as a dogma by monotheistic religion. It is the idea of the one. All knowledge and understanding rest upon its validity. In spite of the profound differences in what it describes and means in the various realms of human thought, there is much that is common and much that is of mutual importance.

THE IDEA OF THE UNIVERSE

The perspective on which we depend in science and philosophy, notwithstanding all specialization and meticulousness in studying the details, is a view of the whole, without which our knowledge would be like a book composed exclusively of iotas. Accordingly, all sciences and philosophies have one axiom in common—the axiom of *unity* of all that is, was and

* *Nofet Zufim*, 22.

will be. They all assume that things are not entirely divorced from and indifferent to each other, but subject to universal laws, and that they form, by their interaction with one another or, as Lotze put it, by their "sympathetic rapport," a universe. However, the possibility of their interaction with each other is conditioned upon a unity that pervades all of them. The world could not exist at all except as one; deprived of unity, it would not be a cosmos but chaos, an agglomeration of countless possibilities.

The exponents of pluralism, asserting that "reality is made up of a number of relatively independent entities, each of which exists, at any rate to some extent, in its own right," seem to deny the fundamental unity and wholeness of the universe. Yet, while questioning whether that unity is absolute and all-pervading to a degree that would exclude chance and indeterminations, they are bound to supplement the pluralistic hypothesis by a principle of unity, in order to explain the interaction of the independent entities, and to account for that which makes reality a world.*

Nor does the theory of relativity contradict the doctrine of constancy and unity of nature. Showing that the simultaneity of two processes is relative and that magnitudes are determined by the system of reference in which they are measured, its aim is to find new invariants by describing reality in a way which would be independent of the choice of the system of reference. It does not discard the principle of unity, but, on the contrary, strives to "satisfy a new and more strict demand for unity."**

* Cf. C. A. Richardson, *Spiritual Realism and Recent Philosophy*, p. 82f.
** Ernst Cassirer, *Substance and Function and Einstein's Theory of Relativity*, Chicago, 1923, p. 373f.

While it is impossible to trace back the way in which the great secret of the all-embracing unity reached our minds, it certainly was not attained by mere sense perception or by a mind that thought in installments, through a series of distinct steps, each logically dependent on those which preceded. What the idea of the universe refers to surpasses the scope of perception or the extension of any possible premise, embracing things known and unknown, origins and ends, facts and possibilities, the prehistoric past and the far-stretching future, phenomena which Newton described as well as those which will be observed a thousand years from now. The idea of the universe is a metaphysical insight.

COSMIC BROTHERHOOD

The intuition of that all-pervading unity has often inspired man with a sense of living in cosmic brotherhood with all beings. Out of the awareness of the oneness of nature comes often an emotion of being one with nature.

> I am the eye with which the Universe
> Beholds itself and knows itself divine.
> (Shelley "Hymn of Apollo" vi. lf)

There is deep philosophical significance to such cosmic piety. Knowledge is at all possible because of the kinship of the knower and the known, because man's intelligence seems to correspond to the world's intelligibility. But over and above that there is another kinship: the kinship of being. We are all—men, stars, flowers, birds—assigned to the same cast, rehearsing for the same inexplicable drama. We all have a mystery in common—the mystery of being.

But are we all *one* in purpose? True, we all have being, even suffering and a struggle for existence in common; but do we have strivings, commitments in common? Man's position in nature is too distinct to justify the idea that his vocation is to conform to her ways or to be one with her essence.

THE REALM OF BEING AND THE REALM OF VALUES

The idea of unity, from which cosmic piety draws its inspiration, is a half-truth. For while the things of nature may constitute a unit, the realm of values seems to be torn between good and evil and in many other directions. History is no less our abode than nature, and the conflicts that rage within it look more like perennial warfare between two hostile principles than like a sphere of harmony.

It is, indeed, a spiritual temptation to meditate on the cosmic fellowship of all beings or to surrender once and for all to the spirit of the whole. It is suspiciously easier to feel one with nature than to feel one with every man: with the savage, with the leper, with the slave. Those who know that to be one with the whole means to be for the sake of every part of the whole will seek to love not only humanity but also the individual man, to regard any man as if he were all men. Once we decide to serve here and now, we discover that the vision of abstract unity goes out of sight like lightning, and what remains is the gloom of a drizzly night, where we must in toil and tears strike the darkness to beget a gleam, to light a torch.

Polytheists are blind to the unity that transcends a world of multiplicity, while monists overlook the multiplicity of a world, the abundance and discord of which encounter us wherever we turn. Monism is a loom for weaving an illusion. Life is tangled, fierce, fickle. We cannot remain in agreement with all goals. We are constantly compelled to make a choice, and the choice of one goal means the forsaking of another.

Even granted its validity, the idea of a universal harmony in nature, of a general concord in the relations of the part to the whole is destitute of significance to the immediate problems of living. However intricate, wise and prodigal of beauty nature is, we in our human confusions are unable to translate its general laws into the language of individual decisions, for to decide means to transcend rather than follow the pattern of natural laws. The norms of spiritual living are a challenge to nature not a part of nature. There is a discrepancy between being and spirit, between facts and norms, between that which is and that which ought to be. Nature shows little regard for spiritual norms and is often callous, if not hostile to our moral endeavors.

Man is more than reason. Man is life. In facing the all-embracing question, he faces that which is more than a principle, more than a theoretical problem. A principle is something he may conceive or convert into an object of his mind, but in facing the ultimate question man finds himself called upon and challenged beyond words to the depth of his existence. It is not a question that he comprehends but the fact of his being exposed to a knowledge that comprehends him. Of what avail, then, is the knowledge of principles, the mathematical principles?

Man is not alone

God is one, but one is not God. Some of us are inclined to deify the one supreme force or law that regulates all phenomena of nature, in the same manner in which primitive peoples once deified the stars. Yet, to refer to the supreme law of nature as God or to say that the world came into being by virtue of its own energy is to beg the question.

For the cardinal question is not what is the law that would explain the interaction of phenomena in the universe, but why is there a law, a universe at all. The content and operation of the universal law may be conceived and described, but the fact that there is such a law does not lose its ineffable character by the knowledge we may acquire about the scope of its operation.

To instill scientific explanations of nature in a soul astir with the holy terror of the ineffable is like trying to plant artificial flowers in the midst of blossoms in a garden. Unless we betray what we sense, unless we succumb to intellectual narcissism, how can we regard the known as the ultimate?

As noted above, it is not nature's order and wisdom which are manifest in time and space, but the indicativeness within all order and wisdom of that which surpasses them, of that which is beyond time and space which communicates to us an awareness of the ultimate questions. The world is replete with such indicativeness; wherever we go it is the ineffable we encounter, with our sense too feeble and unworthy to grasp it. If the universe is an immense allusion and our inner life an anonymous quotation, the discovery of one universal law dominating empirical reality would not answer our essential question. The ultimate problem is not a problem of syntax, of trying to learn how the various parts of nature are collocated and arranged in their relations to one another. The problem is: What does reality, what does unity stand for? Universal laws one attempts to describe by relations within the given, within the known, but in facing our ultimate question we are carried beyond the known, to the presence of the divine.

From the empirical plurality of facts and values, we could not infer *one* design which would dominate both the realm of facts and the realm of norms, nature and history. It is only in the mirror of a divine unity, in which we may behold the unity of all: of necessity and freedom, of law and love. It alone gives us an insight into the unity that transcends all conflicts, the brotherhood of hope and grief, of joy and fear, of tower and grave, of good and evil. Unity as a scientific concept is only a reflection of a transcendent idea, embracing not only time and space but also being and value, the known and the mystery, the here and the beyond.

God cannot be distilled to a well-defined idea. All concepts fade when applied to His essence. To the pious man knowledge of God is not a thought within his grasp, but a form of thinking in which he tries to comprehend all reality. It is the untold secret of the soil in which all knowledge becomes a seed of sense, a secret by which we live and which we never truly understand; a soil from which the roots of all values derive perpetual vitality. Over and against the split between man and nature, self and thought, time and timelessness, the pious man is able to sense the interweaving of all, the holding together of what is apart, the love that hovers over acts of kindness, mountains, flowers, which shine in their splendor as if looked at by God.

How do we identify the divine?

Divine is a message that discloses unity where we see diversity, that discloses peace when we are involved in discord. God is He who holds our fitful lives together, who reveals to us that what is empirically diverse in color, in interest, in creeds—races, classes, nations—is one in His eyes and one in essence.

God means: No one is ever alone; the essence of the temporal is the eternal; the moment is an image of eternity in an infinite mosaic. God means: *Togetherness of all beings in holy otherness.*

God means: What is behind our soul is beyond our spirit; what is at the source of our selves is at the goal of our ways. He is the heart of all, eager to receive and eager to give.

When God becomes our form of thinking we begin to sense all men in one man, the whole world in a grain of sand, eternity in a moment. To worldly ethics one human being is less than two human beings, to the religious mind if a man has caused a single soul to perish, it is as though he had caused a whole world to perish, and if he has saved a single soul, it is as though he had saved a whole world.*

If in the afterglow of a religious insight I can see a way to gather up my scattered life, to unite what lies in strife; a way that is good for all men as it is for me—I will know it is His way.

* Mishnah Sanhedrin, 4, 5.

13 One God

It is strange that modern students of religion fail to realize the constant necessity for the protest against polytheism. The idea of unity is not only one upon which the ultimate justification of philosophical, ethical and religious universalism depends, but also one which is still beyond the grasp of most people. Monotheism, to this day, is at variance with vulgar thinking; it is something against which popular instinct continues to rebel. Polytheism seems to be more compatible with emotional moods and imagination than uncompromising monotheism, and great poets have often felt drawn to pagan gods. The world over, polytheism exercises an almost hypnotic appeal, stirring up powerful, latent yearnings for pagan forms; for it is obviously easier to an average mind to worship under polytheistic than under monotheistic thought.

Yet, while popular and even poetic imagination is fascinated by a vision of ultimate pluralism, metaphysical thought as well as scientific reflection is drawn to the concept of unity.

UNITY AS A GOAL

It is impossible to ignore the patent fact that unity is that which the uninterrupted advance of knowledge and experience leads us to, whether or not we are consciously striving for it. In our own age we have been forced into the realization that, in terms of human relations, there will be either one world or no world. But political and moral unity as a goal presupposes unity as a source; the brotherhood of men would be an empty dream without the fatherhood of God.

Eternity is another word for unity. In it, past and future are not apart; here is everywhere, and now goes on forever. The opposite of eternity is diffusion not time. Eternity does not begin when time is at its end. Time is eternity broken in space, like a ray of light refracted in the water.

The vision of the unbroken ray above the water, the craving for unity and coherence, is the predominant feature of a mature mind. All science, all philosophy, all art are a search after it. But unity is a task, not a condition. The world lies in strife, in discord, in divergence. Unity is beyond, not within, reality.* We all crave it. We are all animated by a passionate will to endure; and to endure means to be *one*.

The world is *not* one with God, and this is why His power does not surge unhampered throughout all stages of being. Creature is detached from the Creator, and the universe is in a state of spiritual disorder. Yet God has not withdrawn entirely from this world. The spirit of this unity hovers over the face of all plurality, and the major trend of all our thinking and striving is its mighty intimation. The goal of all efforts is to bring about the restitution of the unity of God and world. The restoration of that unity is a constant process and its accomplishment will be the essence of Messianic redemption.

* "Thou art He who ties them together and unites them; and aside from Thee there is no unity either above or below" (Second Introduction to *Tikkune Zohar*).

Man is not alone

Xenophones, looking at the universe, said: "All is one." Parmenides, in taking the one seriously, was bound to deny the reality of everything else. Moses, however, did not say: "All is one," but: "God is One." Within the world there is the stubborn fact of plurality, divergence and conflict: "See, I have set before thee this day life and good, death and evil" (Deuteronomy 30:15). But God is the origin of all:

> I am the Lord, and there is none else;
> Beside Me there is no God . . .
> I am the Lord, and there is none else;
> I form the light, and create darkness;
> I make peace, and create evil;
> I am the Lord, that doeth all these things.
>
> (Isaiah 45:5-7)

WHITHER SHALL I GO . . .

The vision of the One, upon which we stake our effort and our ultimate hope, is not to be found in contemplations about nature or history. It is a vision of Him who transcends the scenes of both, subdued yet present everywhere, giving us the power to aid in bringing about ultimate unification.

> Whither shall I go from Thy spirit?
> Or whither shall I flee from Thy presence?
> If I ascend up into heaven, Thou art there;
> If I make my bed in the netherworld, behold, Thou art there . . .

113

And if I say: Surely the darkness shall envelope me,
And the Light about me shall be night,
Even the darkness is not too dark for Thee . . .

(Psalms 139:8-12)

Mythopoeic thought is drawn to the beauty of the sparkling waves, their relentless surge and tantalizing rhythm. Abiding in the fragment, it accepts the instrumental as the final, it has an image, an expression that corresponds to its experience. In contrast, he who takes the ineffable seriously is not infatuated with the fraction. To his mind there is no power in the world which could bear the air of divinity.

Nothing we can count, divide or surpass—a fraction or plurality—can be taken as the ultimate. Beyond two is one. Plurality is incompatible with the sense of the ineffable. You cannot ask in regard to the divine: Which one? There is only one synonym for God: One.

To the speculative mind the oneness of God is an idea inferred from the idea of the ultimate perfection of God; to the sense of the ineffable the oneness of God is self-evident.

HEAR, O ISRAEL

Nothing in Jewish life is more hallowed than the saying of the Shema: "Hear, O Israel, the Lord is our God, the Lord is One." All over the world "the people acclaim His Oneness evening and morning, twice every day, and with tender affection recite the Shema" (Kedusha of Musaf on the Shabbath). The voice that calls: "Hear, He is One," is recalled, revived. It is the climax of devotion at the close of the Day of Atonement. It is the last word to come from the lips of the dying Jew and from the lips of those who are present at that moment.

Yet, ask an average Jew what the adjective "one" means, and he will tell you its negative meaning—it denies the existence of many deities. But is such a negation worth the price of martyrdom which Israel was so often willing to pay for it? Is there no positive content in it to justify the unsurpassed dignity which the idea of One God has attained in Jewish history? Furthermore, doubts have been raised whether the term "one" is at all meaningful when applied to God. For how can we designate Him by a number? A number is one of a series of symbols used in arranging quantities, in order to set them in a relation to one another. Since God is not in time or space, not a part of a series, "the term 'one' is just as inapplicable to God as the term 'many'; for both unity and plurality are categories of quantity, and are, therefore, as inapplicable to God as crooked and straight in reference to sweetness, or salted and insipid in reference to a voice" (Maimonides, *The Guide of the Perplexed*, I, 57).

The boldness of coming out against all deities, against the sanctities of all nations, had more behind it than the abstraction: "One, not many." Behind that revolutionary statement: "All the gods of the nations are vanities," was a new insight into the relation of the divine to nature: "but He made the heavens" (Psalms 96:5). In paganism the deity was a part of nature, and worship was an element in man's relation to nature. Man and his deities were both subjects of nature. Monotheism in teaching that God is the Creator, that nature and man are both fellow-creatures of God, redeemed man from exclusive allegiance to nature. The earth is our sister, not our mother.

The young lions roar after their prey,
And seek their food from God . . .
Living creatures, both small and great . . .
All of them wait for Thee,
That Thou mayest give them their food in due season.

(Psalms 104:21, 25, 27)

The heavens are not God, they are His witnesses: they declare His glory.

ONE MEANS UNIQUE

One in the meaning of "One, not many," is but the beginning of a series of meanings. Its metaphysical incongruousness with the spiritual idea of God notwithstanding, it stands forever like a barrier to prevent the flow of polytheistic nonsense that always threatens to devastate the minds of men. Yet the true meaning of divine unity is not in His being one in a series, one among others. Monotheism was not attained by means of numerical reduction, by bringing down the multitude of deities to the smallest possible number. One means *unique*.

The minimum of knowledge is the knowledge of God's uniqueness.* His being unique is an aspect of His being ineffable.

---

* In Hebrew the word *ehad* means both one and unique. It is in the latter sense in which *ehad* is to be understood in the passage of II Samuel 7:23, incorporated in the afternoon service for the Sabbath: "Thou art One and Thy name is One; and who is like Thy people Israel unique (*ehad*) on earth." This was also the understanding of the rabbis, cf. Bechorot 6b. The Targum renders *ehad* with "unique" in Genesis 26:10. *Ehad* is taken in the sense of *meyuhad*, i.e., "unique," unlike other beings, in Megillah 28a. In rabbinic literature God is

To say He is more than the universe would be like saying that eternity is more than a day.

Of this I am sure: His essence is different from all I am able to know or say. He is not only superior, He is incomparable. There is no equivalent of the divine. He is not "an aspect of nature," not an additional reality, existing along with this world, but a reality that is over and above the universe.

> He is One, and there is no other
> To compare to Him, to place beside him.
>> (Yigdal)

> With whom will ye compare Me
> That I should be similar?
> Saith the Holy One.
>> (Isaiah 40:25)

The Creator cannot be likened to what He created:

> Lift up your eyes on high,
> And see: who hath created these?
>> (Isaiah 40:26)

ONE MEANS ONLY

God is one means He alone is truly real. One means exclusively, no one else, no one besides, alone, only. In I Kings 4:19, as well as in other biblical passages, *ehad* means "only." Significantly the etymology of the English word "only" is one-ly.

---

sometimes called *Yehido shel olam*, the Unique of the universe, or *Yahid be-olamo*, cf. Tanhuma Buber I, 49a: "because God is unique in the universe, He knows the character of every single creature and their minds!" Compare also Hullin 28a, 83b; Bechorot 17a.

"What are we? What is our life? What is our goodness? What our righteousness? What our helpfulness? What our strength? What our might? What can we say in Thy presence, Lord our God and God of our fathers? Indeed, all the heroes are as nothing before Thee, the men of renown as though they never existed, the wise as if they were without knowledge, the intelligent as though they lacked understanding; for most of their doings are worthless, and the days of their life are vain in Thy sight" (Morning Service).

God is One; He alone is real. "All the nations are as nothing before Him; they are accounted by Him as things of nought, and vanity" (Isaiah 40:17).

"For we must needs die, and as water spilt on the ground which cannot be gathered up again" (II Samuel 14:14).

ONE MEANS THE SAME

The speculative mind can only formulate isolated questions, asking at times: What is the origin of all being? and at other times: What is the meaning of existence? To the sense of the ineffable there is only one question, extending beyond all categories of expression, aspects of which are reflected in such questions as: Who created the world? Who rules the history of man? And Israel's answer is: One God. One denotes inner unity: His law *is* mercy; His mercy *is* law.*

"One" in this sense signifies "the same." This is the true meaning of "God is One." He is a being who is both beyond and here, both in nature and in history, both love and power,

* See the note on p. 148.

118

near and far, known and unknown, Father and Eternal. The
true concept of unity is attained only in knowing that there is
one being who is both Creator and Redeemer; "I am the Lord,
thy God, who brought thee out of the land of Egypt" (Exodus
20:2). It is this declaration of the *sameness*, of the identity of
the Creator and the Redeemer, with which the Decalogue begins.*

> They depicted Thee in countless visions;
> Despite all comparisons Thou art One.
> *(The Hymn of Glory)*

His is only a single way: His power is His love, His justice
is His mercy. What is divergent to us is one in Him. This is a
thought to which we may apply the words of Ibn Gabirol:

> Thou art One
> And none can penetrate . . .
> The mystery of Thy unfathomable unity . . .
> (Ibn Gabirol, *Keter Malhut*)

GOOD AND EVIL

Moral sentiments do not originate in reason as such. A most
learned man may be wicked, while a plain unlettered man may
be righteous. Moral sentiments originate in man's sense of
unity, in his appreciation of what is common to men. Perhaps

* The Decalogue does not represent, as some scholars assert, a tribal
henotheism in the sense that the tribe of Israel should recognize Him
alone without denying the reality of the deities that other tribes continued to worship; a God, of whom no image should be made, who
created "heaven and earth, the sea, and all that in them is" (Exodus
20:11), cannot admit the reality of other deities.

the most fundamental statement of ethics is contained in the words of the last prophet of Israel: "Have we not all one Father? Has not one God made us? Then why do we break faith with one another, every man with his fellow, by dishonouring our time-honoured troth?" (Malachi 2:10). The ultimate principle of ethics is not an imperative but an ontological fact. While it is true that what distinguishes a moral attitude is the consciousness of obligation to do it, yet an act is not good because we feel obliged to do it; it is rather that we feel obliged to do it because it is good.

The essence of a moral value is neither in its being valid independent of our will nor in its claim that it ought to be done for its own sake. These characteristics refer only to our attitude to such values rather than to their essence. They, furthermore, express an aspect that applies to logical or esthetic values as well.

Seen from God, the good is identical with life and organic to the world; wickedness is a disease, and evil identical with death. For evil is *divergence*, confusion, that which *alienates* man from man, man from God, while good is *convergence*, togetherness, *union*. Good and evil are not qualities of the mind but relations within reality. Evil is division, contest, lack of unity, and as the unity of all being is prior to the plurality of things, so is the good prior to evil.

Good and evil persist regardless of whether or not we pay attention to them. We are not born into a vacuum, but stand, *nolens volens*, in relations to all men and to one God. Just as we do not create the dimensions of space in order to construct geometrical figures, so we do not create the moral and the spiritual relations; they are given with existence. All we do is try to find our way in them. The good does not begin in the consciousness of man. It is being realized in the natural co-operation of all beings, in what they are for each other.

Neither stars nor stones, neither atoms nor waves, but their belonging together, their interaction, the relation of all things to one another constitutes the universe. No cell could exist alone, all bodies are interdependent, affect and serve one another. Figuratively speaking, even rocks bear fruit, are full of unappreciated kindness, when their strength holds up a wall.

HE IS ALL EVERYWHERE

Rabbi Moshe of Kobrin said once to his disciples: "Do you want to know where God is?" He took a piece of bread from the table, showed it to everybody and said: "Here is God." *

In saying God is everywhere, we do not intend to say He is like the air, the parts of which are found in countless places. One in a metaphysical sense means wholeness, indivisibility. God is not partly here and partly there; He is all here and all there.

> Lord, where shall I find thee?
> High and hidden is thy place;
> And where shall I not find thee?
> The world is full of thy glory.
>   (Jehudah Halevi)

"Can any hide himself in secret places that I shall not see him? saith the Lord. Do not I fill heaven and earth? saith the Lord" (Jeremiah 23:24).

* *Or Yesharim,* 87.

God is within all things, not only in the life of man. "Why did God speak to Moses from the thornbush?" was a question a pagan asked of a rabbi. To the pagan mind He should have appeared upon a lofty mountain or in the majesty of a thunderstorm. And the rabbi answered: "To teach you that there is no place on earth where the Shechinah is not, not even a humble thornbush" (Exodus Rabba 2:9; cf. Song of Songs Rabba 3:16). Just as the soul fills the body, so God fills the world. Just as the soul carries the body so God carries the world. *

The natural and the supernatural are not two different spheres, detached from one another as heaven from earth. God is not beyond but right here; not only close to my thoughts but also to my body. This is why man is taught to be aware of His presence, not only by prayer, study and meditation but also in his physical demeanor, by how and what to eat and drink, by keeping the body free from whatever sullies and defiles.

"An idol is near and far; God is far and near" (Deuteronomy Rabba 2:6). "God is far, and yet nothing is closer than He." "He is near with every kind of nearness" (Jerushalmi Berachot 13a).

It is His otherness, ineffable and immediate as the air we breathe and do not see, which enables us to sense His distant nearness. "For thus saith the high and lofty One that inhabiteth eternity, whose name *is* Holy; I dwell in the high and holy place, with him also that is of a contrite and humble spirit, to revive the spirit of the humble, and to revive the heart of the contrite ones" (Isaiah 57:15).

* Leviticus Rabba 4, 8; Deuteronomy Rabba 2, 26; cf. Berachot 10b.

Man is not alone

Unity of God is power for unity of God with all things. He is one in Himself and striving to be one with the world. Rabbi Samuel ben Ammi remarked that the Biblical narrative of creation proclaims: "One day . . . a second day . . . a third day," and so on. If it is a matter of time reckoning, we would expect the Bible to say: "One day . . . two days . . . three days" or: "The first day . . . the second day . . . the third day," but surely not one, second, third!

Yom ehad, one day, really means the day which God desired to be *one* with man. "From the beginning of creation the Holy One, blessed be He, longed to enter into partnership with the terrestrial world." * The unity of God is a concern for the unity of the world.

* Genesis Rabba ch. 3, 9; see p. 243.

14 God Is the Subject

The world to the human self is a world thought of by his self. But is the human self which has entered the world at a late hour in eternity's time an unprecedented pioneer in trying to blaze a path in a spiritual void, in trying to create ideas out of nothing, music out of chaos? Is the human mind a glowworm in the dark, attempting all alone to illumine the wide expanse of eternity?

Only he who lives in a prison of conceit can claim that man is alone and the only one who knows. Anyone whose mind is not detached from his sense of the ineffable will find it impossible to conceive that man has the preemptory power to think to the exclusion of any other spirit, as if the world were unpremeditated, its meaning-qualities precarious, depending exclusively on the mind of man. It is *absurd* even though it may be *conceivable* to assume that man is the only being endowed with mental and spiritual abilities.

Man is never the first in thinking about any being, in performing that strange operation of converting a thing into an object of thought; at least, he does not consider himself to be the first. The explorer, obtaining the first glimpse of an unknown island, cannot believe that all the beauty and grandeur he encountered had never been seen, never thought of, never

125

appreciated, until he arrived. In the daily routine of thinking it seems to us that the self is the only active factor, the only power that counts; the world is just material to be utilized. And so are ideas—commodities to be expended and consumed according to desire. It is different in the life of independent, creative souls who approach the world not as self-inflated masters, as self-celebrating subjects. They abandon all they know to become receptive, to become a focus in which the luminousness of the world may be captured. Creative insight is not brought about by computations. It comes as a response within an experience in which the meaning of things imposes its force upon the experient.

To the sense of the ineffable the world is not virgin soil. The world *is* and is *thought* of. Eternity is the memory of God. The world stands in front of us, while God walks behind us.

The more deeply alert we become to the inwardness in which all things are engrossed and to the mystery of being which we share with all things, the more deeply we realize the object-nature of the self. We begin to understand that what is an "I" to our minds is an "it" to God. This is why object-consciousness rather than self-consciousness is the starting point for our thoughts about Him. It is in our object-consciousness that we first learn to understand that God is more than the divine.

THE THOUGHT OF GOD HAS NO FAÇADE

Accustomed to thinking in categories of space, we conceive of God as being vis-à-vis ourselves, as if we were here and He were there. We think of Him in the likeness of things, as if He were a thing among things, a being among beings.

Entering the meditation about the ultimate, we must rid ourselves of the intellectual habit of converting reality into an object of our minds. Thinking of God is totally different from thinking about all other matters; to apply the usual logical devices would be like trying to blow away a tempest with a breath. We often fail in trying to understand Him, not because we do not know how to extend our concepts far enough, but because we do not know how to begin close enough. To think of God is not to find Him as an object in our minds, but to find ourselves in Him. Religion begins where experience ends, and the end of experience is a perception of our being perceived.

To have knowledge of a thing is to have its concept at our mind's disposal. Since concept and thing, definition and essence belong to different realms, we are able to conquer and to own a thing theoretically, while the thing itself may be away from us, as is the case, for example, in our knowledge of stellar nebulae.

God is neither a thing nor an idea; He is within and beyond all things and all ideas. Thinking of God is not beyond but within Him. The thought of Him would not be in front of us, if God were not behind it.

The thought of God has no façade. We are all in it as soon as it is all in us. To conceive it is to be absorbed by it, like the present in the past, in a past that never dies.

Our knowing Him and His reality are not apart. To think of Him is to open our minds to His all-pervading presence, to our being replete with His presence. To think of things means to have a concept within the mind, while to think of Him is

like walking under a canopy of thought, like being surrounded by thought. He remains beyond our reach as long as
we do not know that our reach is within Him; that He is the
Knower and we are the known; that to be means to be thought
of by Him.

Thinking of God is made possible by His being the *subject*
and by our being His *object*. To think of God is to expose
ourselves to Him, to conceive ourselves as a reflection of His
reality. He cannot be limited to a thought. To think means to
set aside or to separate an object from the thinking subject.
But in setting Him apart, we gain an idea and lose Him. Since
He is not away from us and we are not beyond Him, He can
never become the mere object of our thought. As, in thinking
about ourselves, the object cannot be detached from the subject, so in thinking of God the subject cannot be detached
from the object. In thinking of Him, we realize that it is
through Him that we think of Him. Thus, we must think of
Him as the subject of all, as the life of our life, as the mind of
our mind.

If an idea had ability to think and to transcend itself, it
would be aware of its being at this moment a thought of my
mind. The religious man has such an awareness of being
known by God, as if he were an object, a thought in His
mind.

To the philosopher God is an *object*, to men at prayer He
is the *subject*. Their aim is not to possess Him as a concept of
knowledge, to be informed about Him, as if He were a fact
among facts. What they crave for is to be wholly possessed
by Him, to be an object of His knowledge and to sense it. The
task is not to know the unknown but to be penetrated with it;
not to know but *to be known* to Him, to expose ourselves to

Him rather than Him to us; not to judge and to assert but to listen and to be judged by Him.

His knowledge of man precedes man's knowledge of Him, while man's knowledge of Him comprehends only what God asks of man. This is the essential content of prophetic revelation.*

GOD'S VISION OF MAN

The Bible is primarily not man's vision of God but God's vision of man. The Bible is not man's theology but God's anthropology, dealing with man and what He asks of him rather than with the nature of God. God did not reveal to the prophets eternal mysteries but His knowledge and love of man. It was not the aspiration of Israel to know the Absolute but to ascertain what He asks of man; to commune with His will rather than with His essence.

In the depth of our trembling, all that we can utter is the awareness of our being known to God. Man cannot see God, but man can be seen by God. He is not the object of a discovery but the subject of revelation.

There are no concepts which we could appoint to designate the greatness of God or to represent Him to our minds. He is not a being, whose existence could be either confirmed or described by our thoughts. He is a reality, in the face of which, when becoming alive to its meaning, we are overtaken with a feeling of infinite unworthiness.

* See A. Heschel, *Die Prophetie*, Cracow 1936, p. 182.

While modern man has a poor sense of mystery, he is willing to accept a principle of agnosticism as a panacea to all theological and metaphysical problems. He is ready to believe that if there is a supreme being, the difference between Him and man is far greater than the difference between unconscious matter and conscious man; that man, consequently, may know as much about Him as a bubble knows about the theory of relativity; that God has nothing to do with this wretched globe; that He is aloft and so far above the forms of existence known to us that nothingness alone is where He dwells. It is as plausible today to move Him beyond all beyonds as it was once to sense a spirit within a tree or a stone. Yet, he who insists that God is in every way unknowable claims to know that what he says cannot be known. He claims to know that God lives in a jail of inscrutable unrelatedness, behind the bars of infiniteness and wholly otherness.

The term "knowledge," in the sense in which it is used in regard to finite things, is, indeed, inapplicable to the essence of God. Yet, there is more contained in our awareness than the certainty that He exists. If to be immersed in thought means to wear opinions on the head like plumes, then we are witless; but if thoughts are like blood that circulates in us, then they may be found at a sensitive soul's finger tips. We often know Him unknowingly and fail to know Him when insisting upon knowing.

Man is akin to the divine by what he is, not only by what he attains. The essence of his spirit which wrestles with Him who is beyond the ineffable and often prevails must, indeed, be pertinent to God. And if his spirit ever rises to reach out for Him, it is the divine in man that accounts for his exaltation: "The spirit of man is the lamp of the Lord, searching all the inward parts" (Proverbs 20:27).

God would be beyond our reach if we were to search for Him within the maze in the light of our mental fireworks. But we are "dust and ashes"; dust of the earth and ashes from His fire, and the mind, stirring up the soul, may fan the embers of His fire which are still aglow. To ask, then, why we believe, is like asking why we perceive. Our trust in God is God (Deuteronomy Rabba 1, 10).

We do not need words in order to communicate with the mystery. The ineffable in us communes with the ineffable beyond us. We do not have to express God when we let our self continue to be His, the echo of His expression.

Resorting to the divine invested in us, we do not have to bewail the fact of His shore being so far away. In our sincere compliance with His commands, the distance disappears. It is not in our power to force the beyond to become here; but we can transport the here into the beyond.

OUR KNOWLEDGE IS AN UNDERSTATEMENT

Life, as we see it, is not all a wilderness of follies. There are in it both fertility and sterility, both meaning and absurdity. Is it conceivable that wisdom, music, love, order, beauty, holiness have come out of chaos, out of something lifeless, inferior to you and me? Is that startling, unfathomable wealth of spirit the product of an accident? It would be absurd to assume that the power in us which created laws, ideals, symphonies and holiness is contained only in us and exists nowhere else.

No one will deny that there are men who despised the gain of oppression, who shake their hands from holding bribes. Whatever their motives, we all revere their way. Even though we may be unable to attain perfect righteousness, we at least cherish it as an ideal, as the finest of norms, and are even able to implement it to some degree. To assert that such an ideal and its implementation are the monopoly of man and unknown to the Supreme Being, that man is the only being endowed with intellectual and moral qualities, that he is superior to the Supreme Being, is something which is both absurd and revolting, a folly that can be maintained only as long as man sees only himself and his specious glory, and dissipates with the first glance at his true situation. He who ever has sensed the endless superiority of the ineffable is wise enough to admit that God cannot be inferior to any other being, that we could not own the power for goodness if it were lacking in God. If there is morality in us, it must eminently be in God. If we possess the vision of justice, it must eminently be in God. Even the cry of despair: There is no justice in heaven!—is a cry in the name of justice, a justice that cannot have come out of us and still be missing in the source of ourselves. He who is alive to the ineffable will refuse to accept a source of energy called the first cause as expressing the highest. He knows that to assert that the highest is endowed with spirit is a gross understatement; that rather than formulate it, he would seek to hide in silence . . .

Man is not alone

It is more appropriate to describe the ideas we acquire in our wrestling with the ineffable as understanding of God. For if He is neither an abstract principle nor a thing, but a unique living being, our approach to Him cannot be through the procedures of knowledge but through a process of understanding. We know through induction or inference, we understand through intuition; we know a thing, we understand a personality; we know a fact, we understand a hint. Knowledge implies familiarity with, or even the mastery of, something; understanding is an act of interpreting something which we only know by its expression and through inner agreement with it. There is no sympathetic knowledge but there is sympathetic understanding. Understanding, significantly, is a synonym for agreement. It is through agreement that we find a way of understanding.

The ineffable we may know and recognize. Yet only rarely do men learn how to live in ultimate agreement, and this is why they so often miss the way which leads from the ineffable to Him. In the prophets the ineffable became a voice, disclosing that God is not a being that is apart and away from ourselves, as ancient man believed, that He is not an enigma, but justice, mercy; not only a power to which we are accountable, but also a pattern for our lives. He is not the Unknown, He is the Father, the God of Abraham; out of stillness of endless ages came compassion and guidance.

15 The Divine Concern

It is a familiar finale—after thought opposed thought, argument collided with argument, philosophers would arrive at the solemn conclusion: We cannot know *what* He is, we only know *that* He is; which means: We know nothing about His attributes, all we can ascribe to Him is *existence*. But admittedly, existence is an indefinable concept, it cannot be imagined *per se*, unqualified, in utter nakedness; it is always some particular, specific existent, or a mode of existence, a being dressed in attributes, that we grasp. Thus, all that such speculation about God brings forth is an ineffable category. Existence is, moreover, not only the end, but also the starting point of all thinking about God, for without assuming the possibility of His being in existence, we would not begin to contemplate Him.

In their eagerness to avoid the possibility of ascribing anthropomorphic features to God, philosophers have traditionally adopted the procedure prevalent in general ontology, in which the notion of existence that served as a subject matter of analysis was derived from the realm of inanimate rather than from the realm of animate and personal existence. The subsequent efforts to fill the ontological shell with spiritual or moral content have encountered insurmountable difficulties, primarily because of the disparity of inanimate, animate and spiritual existence.

A pencil, a pigeon and a poet have being in common; not only their essence but their existence is not the same. The difference between the existence of a human being and the existence of a pencil is as radical and intrinsic as the difference between the existence of the pencil and the nonexistence of the Flying Dutchman. This becomes apparent when we compare a living man with a corpse. They both contain the same chemical elements in exactly the same proportions, at least immediately after death. Yet a man who is dead is nonexistent as a man, as a human or social being, although he is still existent as a corpse.

LIFE IS CONCERN

Temporality and uninterruptedness express, as we shall see,* the relation of existence to time, a passive relation. What distinguishes organic from inorganic existence is the fact that the plant or the animal stands in an active and defensive relation to temporality. All finite existence, a stone or a dog, is constantly on the verge of nonexistence: any moment it may cease to exist. But unlike the stone, the dog is endowed to a degree with the ability to fight or avoid the ills of life.

Life, we know from biology, is not a passive state of indifference and inertia. The essence of life is intense care and concern. For example, the life of the cell depends upon its

* See p. 200 ff.

136

power to manufacture and to retain certain substances that are necessary to its survival. These substances are prevented from diffusing out, because the outer surface of the cell is impermeable to them. At the same time, this surface, owing to the selective permeability of the protoplasm, allows other favorable substances to penetrate into the cell from the outside, while refusing admission to substances that are unfavorable. Every cell behaves like an accordion, contracting when brought into contact with something destructive. On the basis of these observations the following biological principle may be established: every living organism abhors its own destruction.

We may, therefore, say that just as the peculiar quality of inorganic existence is necessity and inertia, the peculiar asset of organic existence, or life, is concern. Life *is* concern.

Such concern is reflexive: it refers to one's own self and is rooted in the anxiety of the self about its own future. If man paid no attention to the future, if he were indifferent to that which may or may not come, he would not know any anxiety. The past is gone, at present he is alive, it is only the time to come of which he is apprehensive.

THE TRANSITIVE CONCERN

A man entirely unconcerned with his self is dead; a man exclusively concerned with his self is a beast. The mark of distinction from the beast as well as the index of maturity is the tridimensionality of man's concern. The child becomes human, not by discovering the environment which includes things and other selves, but by becoming sensitive to the interests of other selves. Human is he who is concerned with other selves. Man is a being that can never be self-sufficient, not only by what he must take in but also by what he must give out. A stone is self-sufficient, man is self-surpassing. Always in need of other beings to give himself to, man cannot even be in accord with his own self unless he serves something beyond himself. The peace of mind attainable in solitude is not the result of ignoring that which is not the self or escaping from it, but of reconciliation with it. The range of needs increases with the rise of the form of existence: a stone is more self-sufficient than a plant, and a horse requires more for its survival than a tree. A vital requirement of human life is transitive concern, a regard for others, in addition to a reflexive concern, an intense regard for itself.

At first the other selves are considered as means to attain the fulfillment of his own needs. The shift from the animal to the human dimension takes place when, as a result of various events, such as observing other people's suffering, falling in love or by being morally educated, he begins to acknowledge the other selves as ends, to respond to their needs even regardless of personal expediency. It is an act of *de jure* or even *de facto* recognition of other human beings as equals, as a result of which he becomes concerned with their concern; what is of importance to them becomes vital to him. Cain when asked about the whereabouts of his brother, gave answer: "Am I my brother's keeper?" (Genesis 4:9). Abraham, unasked, unsolicited, pleaded for Sodom, the city of wickedness. But why was Abraham interested in saving Sodom? Abraham could plead with God for Sodom because there is eternal, unconditional justice, in the name of which he was able to say: "Far be it from Thee to slay the righteous with the wicked . . . Shall not the judge of all the earth do justice?" (Genesis 18:25).

It is not a mechanical, lateral extension of the concern for oneself that brings about the concern for others. The concern for others often demands the price of self-denial. How could self-denial or even self-extinction be explained as a self-extension? Consequently, we cannot say that the concern for others lies on the same level as the concern for oneself, consisting merely in substituting another self for one's own. The motivation of our transitive concern may be selfish. The fact of our transitive concern is not.

THE THREE DIMENSIONS

The concern for others is not an extension in breadth but an ascension, a rise. Man reaches a new vertical dimension, the dimension of the holy, when he grows beyond his self-interests, when that which is of interest to others becomes vital to him, and it is only in this dimension, in the understanding of its perennial validity, that the concern for other human beings and the devotion to ideals may reach the degree of self-denial. Distant ends, religious, moral and artistic interests, may become as relevant to man as his concern for food. The self, the fellow-man and the dimension of the holy are the *three* dimensions of a mature human concern.

True love of man is clandestine love of God. But why? What bearing has the affection or the kindness of one man for another upon the mystery of all mysteries? Should we not dismiss the proverb:

139

He that oppresses the poor reviles his Maker:
He honors his Maker who is gracious to the needy.

(Proverbs 14:31)

as rant and reverie? Is there anything intrinsic in the existence
of God that would justify such a correlation?

Moreover, are we right in saying that man is capable of rising beyond himself? Does not any honest self-analysis reveal
how the motivations of our conduct are entangled in the functions of instinctual desires, how the vested interests of the ego
penetrate our moral motivations as well as our acts of cognition? And yet, while granting all this, it would be wrong to
regard our concern for others as self-concern in disguise.

A COERCION TO FORGET ONESELF

It is not true that man is condemned to life imprisonment in a
realm wherein causality, struggle for existence, will to power,
libido sexualis and the craving for prestige are the only springs
of action. He is involved in relations which run beyond that
realm. There is no man who does not strive, at one time or
another, for some degree of disinterestedness; who does not
seek something to which he could be attached regardless of
advantage. It is not true that all men are at all times at the
mercy of their ego, that promoting their own prosperity is
all they can do. It is not true that in the conflicts of honesty
and expediency the first is always defeated. In every soul there
lives incognito a coercion to love, to forget oneself, to be independent of vested interests. It is against his selfish interests
that man yields to the coercion to brood over purpose, mean-

ing or value of living; that he insists upon judging himself by nonselfish standards and is concerned with ends he does not even fully comprehend; that he often resists the tempting rewards of wealth, power or vulgar popularity; that he foregoes the approval or favor of those who dominate the financial, political or academic world for the sake of remaining loyal to a moral or religious principle.

Our first impulse is self-preservation. It is the essence of organic living, and only he who has contempt for life should condemn it as a vice. If life is holy, as we believe it is, then self-regard is that which maintains the holy. Regard for the self becomes only a vice by association: when associated with complete or partial disregard for other selves. Thus the moral task is not how to disregard one's own self but how to discover and be attentive to another self.

The self is not evil. The precept: "Thou shalt love thy neighbour as thyself," includes the care for one's own self as a duty. It is as mistaken to consider the duty to oneself and the will of God as opposites as it is to identify them. To serve does not mean to surrender but to share.

The statement: "Thou shalt love thy neighbour as thyself," concludes with the words: "I am the Lord." It is this conclusion that contains the ultimate reason for that solemn command. True and timeless is that command; but if God were not God, there would be no truth, no timelessness and no such command.

It is a useless endeavor to fight the ego with intellectual arguments, since like a wounded hydra it produces two heads for every one cut off. Reason alone is incapable of forcing the soul to love or of saying why we ought to love for no profit, for no reward. The great battle for integrity must be fought by aiming at the very heart of the ego and by enhancing the soul's power of freedom.

FREEDOM IS SPIRITUAL ECSTASY

For integrity is the fruit of freedom. The slave will always ask: What will serve my interests? It is the free man who is able to transcend the causality of interest and deed, of act and the desire for personal reward. It is the free man who asks: Why should I be interested in my interests? What are the values I ought to feel in need of serving?

But inner freedom is *spiritual ecstasy*, the state of being beyond all interests and selfishness. Inner freedom is a miracle of the soul. How could such a miracle be achieved?

It is the dedication of the heart and mind to the fact of our being present at a concern of God, the knowledge of being a part of an eternal spiritual movement that conjures power out of a weary conscience, that, striking the bottom out of conceit, tears selfishness to shreds. It is the sense of the ineffable that leads us beyond the horizon of personal interests, helping us to realize the absurdity of regarding the ego as an end.

There is no other way to feel one with every man, with the leper or with the slave, except in feeling one with him in a higher unity: in the one concern of God for all men.

THE DIVINE CONCERN

God's existence—what may it mean? Being eternal, temporality does not apply to Him. May reflexive concern be predicated of

142

Him? He does not have to be concerned about Himself, since there is no need of His being on guard against danger to His existence. The only concern that may be ascribed to Him is a transitive concern, one which is implied in the very concept of creation. For if creation is conceived as a voluntary activity of the Supreme Being, it implies a concern with that which is coming into being. Since God's existence is continuous, His concern or care for His creatures must be abiding. While man's concern for others is often tainted with concern for his own self and characterized as a lack of self-sufficiency and a requirement for the perpetuation of his own existence, God's care for His creatures is a pure concern.

According to Cicero: "The gods are careful about great things and neglect small ones" (*De Natura Deorum*. Book ii. ch. 66, 167). According to the prophets of Israel, from Moses to Malachi, God is concerned with small matters. What the prophets tried to convey to man was not a conception of an eternal harmony, of an unchangeable rhythm of wisdom, but the perception of God's concern with concrete situations. Disclosing the pattern of history, in which the human is interwoven with the divine, they breathed a divine earnestness into the world of man.

In mythology the deities are thought of as self-seeking, as concerned with their own selves. Immortal, superior to man in power and wisdom, they are often inferior to man in morality. "Homer and Hesiod have ascribed to the gods all the things that are a shame and a disgrace among mortals, stealings and adulteries and deceivings of one another" (Xenophones).

The Bible tells us nothing about God in Himself; all its sayings refer to His relations to man. His own life and essence are neither told nor disclosed. We hear of no reflexive concern, of no passions, except a passion for justice. The only events in the life of God the Bible knows of are acts done for the sake of man: acts of creation, acts of redemption (from Ur, from Egypt, from Babylon), or acts of revelation.

Zeus is passionately interested in pretty female deities and becomes inflamed with rage against those who incite his jealousy. The God of Israel is passionately interested in widows and orphans.

Divine concern means His taking interest in the fate of man; it means that the moral and spiritual state of man engages His attention. It is true that His concern is, to most of us, one of the most baffling mysteries, but it is just as true that to those whose life is open to God His care and love are a constant experience.

CONTINUOUS EXPRESSION

In ascribing a transitive concern to God, we employ neither an anthropomorphic nor an anthropopathic concept but an idea that we should like to characterize as an *anthropopneumism* (*anthropo* + *pneuma*). We ascribe to Him not a psychic but a spiritual characteristic, not an emotional but a moral attitude. Those who refuse to ascribe a transitive concern to God are unknowingly compelled to conceive His existence, if it should mean anything at all, after the analogy of physical being and to think of Him in terms of "physiomorphism."

Creation in the language of the Bible is an act of expression. God said: "Let there be"; and it was. And creation is not an act that happened once, but a continuous process. The word

Yehi, "Let there be," stands forever in the universe. If it were not for the presence of that word, there would be no world, there would be finite being (compare Midrash Tehillim, ed. Buber, p. 498).

When we say that He is present within all beings, we do not mean that He inheres in them as a component or ingredient of their physical structure. God in the universe is a spirit of concern for life. What is a thing to us is a concern to God; what is a part of the physical world of being is also a part of a divine world of meaning. *To be* is *to stand for*, to stand for a divine concern.

God is present in His continuous expression. He is immanent in all beings in the way in which a person is immanent in a cry that he utters: He stands for what he says. He is concerned with what he says. All beings are replete with the divine word which only leaves when our viciousness profanes and overbears His silent, patient presence.

It is as easy to expel God as it is to shed blood. And yet even when He hides, even when our souls have lost His trace we may still call Him out of the depths: out of the depths of all things. For God is everywhere save in arrogance.

We may not know *what* He is, but we know *where* He is. No tongue can describe His *essence*, but every soul may both share His *presence* and feel the anguish of His dreadful absence.

Immured in our pompous selfishness, we usually forget where He is, forget that our own self-concern is a cupful drawn from the spirit of divine concern. There is, however, a way of keeping ourselves open to the presence of that spirit. There are moments in which we feel the challenge of a power that, not born of our will nor installed by it, robs us of independence by its judgment of the rectitude or depravity of our actions, by its gnawing at our heart when we offend against its injunctions. It is as if there were no privacy within ourselves, no possibility of either retreat or escape, no place in us in which to bury the remains of our guilt feelings. There is a voice that reaches everywhere, knowing no mercy, digging in the burial places of charitable forgetfulness.

CIVILIZATION HANGS BY A THREAD

The course in which human life moves is, like the orbit of heavenly bodies, an ellipse, not a circle. We are attached to two centers: to the focus of our self and to the focus of God. Driven by two forces, we have both the impulse to acquire, to enjoy, to possess and the urge to respond, to yield, to give.

It seems as though we have arrived at a period of a divine eclipse in human history. We sail the seas, we count the stars, we split the atom, but we never ask: Is there nothing but a dead universe and our reckless curiosity?

Horrified by the discovery of man's power to bring about the annihilation of organic life on this planet, we are today beginning to comprehend that the sense for the sacred is as vital to us as the light of the sun; that the enjoyment of beauty, possessions and safety in civilized society depends upon man's sense for the sacredness of life, upon his reverence for this spark of light in the darkness of selfishness; that once we permit this spark to be quenched, the darkness falls upon us like thunder.

We are impressed by the towering buildings of New York

146

City. Yet not the rock of Manhattan nor the steel of Pittsburgh, but the law that came from Sinai is their ultimate foundation. The true foundation upon which our cities stand is a handful of spiritual ideas. All of our life hangs by a thread —the faithfulness of man to the concern of God.

What is the hope of man with his faithfulness being so feeble, vague, unstable and confused? The world that we have long held in trust has exploded in our hands, and a stream of guilt and misery has been unloosed which leaves no man's integrity unmaimed. But man has become callous to catastrophes. What is our hope with our callousness standing like a wall between our conscience and God?

COMPASSION

Dark is the world to me, for all of its cities and stars, if not for the breath of compassion that God blew in me when he formed me of dust and clay, more compassion than my nerves can bear. God, I am alone with my compassion within my limbs. Dark are my limbs for me; if not for Thee, who could stand such anguish, such disgrace?

"Let me understand Thy ways," Moses prayed. Only weeks had passed since the Hebrew slaves were redeemed from Egypt; only forty days had passed since they heard the Voice proclaiming: "Thou shalt have no other gods besides Me. Thou shalt not make unto thee a graven image," when they made a golden calf. Moses blazed out in anger, flung down the tablets and broke them. Yet, when, following that bitter event, Moses stood again on the top of the mountain with the second tablets in his hand, He came down in a cloud and swept past him, declaring: "God is compassionate and kind, slow to anger, abundant in love and truth, forgiving iniquity, transgression, and sin, but one who will never acquit the guilty, one who visits the iniquity of fathers on their children, and upon their children's children, down to the third and fourth generation." His compassion is not mere emotion; it is blazing with the power of which only He is capable.

When the soul of man is asked: What is God to you? there is only one answer that survives all theories which we carry to the grave: He is full of compassion. The Tetragrammaton, the great Name, we do not know how to pronounce, but we are taught to know what it stands for: "compassion." *

The moral and spiritual adjectives which the Bible ascribes to Him such as *zaddik, hasid, ne'eman,* it also employs in characterizing men who lead good lives. Only one attribute is reserved for God: He alone is called in the Bible *rahum* ** the Merciful One.

God is not all in all. He is in all beings but He is *not* all beings. He is within the darkness but He is not the darkness. His one concern permeates all beings: He is all there, but the absence of the divine is also there. His ends are concealed in the cold facts of nature; His concern is wrapt in the independ-

* It is an old rabbinic doctrine that the Tetragrammaton, usually rendered the Lord, expresses the divine attribute of love, while the name Elohim that of judgment, Sifre Deuteronomy § 27; Pesikta, ed. Buber, pp. 162a and 164a.
** The one exception, Psalm 112:4, is an obvious example of *imitatio Dei,* cf. 111:4. The term is probably related to the word *rehem,* womb, and may have the connotation of motherly love. In the Babylonian Talmud, *Rahmana,* the Merciful One, is frequently used to denote both God and Scripture, Law, or the word of God. The Law *is* Mercy.

ence of the universe which is so well arranged that we are often led to believe that there is no need for occasional repairs. Our perception, therefore, is like listening to a foreign tongue: we perceive the sounds, but miss the meanings. To man, himself but an exclamation in the speech of creation, things seem to function and to behave as if God were an alien whose presence is neither required nor desired. Some of us are haughty and harry the downtrodden. "The ungodly boasts of his rapacity, the plunderer disowns, despises Him; he thinks, in his insolence, 'God never punishes'; all his thoughts are: There is no God at all" (Psalms 10:3-4). Others despair in the fog of the crystal-clear laws of necessity, in which our hopes often freeze to death.

DISPLAY AND DISGUISE

To know of God is not to whistle in the dark, as if exemplifying the world's roaming in impenetrable fog. True, darkness is where we live; yet, though deep and thick, it is neither sordid nor weird. The impenetrable fog in which the world is clad is God's disguise. To know God means to sense display in His disguise and to be aware of the disguise in His most magnificent display.

God is within the world, present and concealed in the essence of things. If not for His presence, there would be no essence; if not for His concealment, there would be no appearance.

The song that nature sings is not her own. She is ablaze with a fire she barely contains; her independence, her unity, her beauty, are borrowed perfection. Only those who do not notice that their knowledge is a pretext for higher ignorance fail to sense the marvel of her fortitude to endure, the marvel of her not being consumed; not seeing the bush, they also miss the voice.

If the universe were explainable as a robot, we could assume that God is separated from it and His relation to it would be like that of a watchmaker to a clock. But the ineffable cries out of all things. It is only the idea of a divine presence hidden within the rational order of nature which is compatible with our scientific view of nature and in accord with our sense of the ineffable.

The soul dwells within, yet the spirit is always hovering above reality. God's infinite concern is present in the world, His essence is transcendent. He includes the universe, but, to quote Solomon's prayer in dedicating the Temple: "Behold, the heaven, and the heaven of heavens, cannot contain Thee" (I Kings 8:27). The awareness of God as the dwelling-place of the universe must have been very poignant in post-Biblical times, if *Makom* ("place") was a synonym for God.

The soul is within: passive, hidden; the spirit is beyond: active, infinite.

16 The Hiding God

For us, contemporaries and survivors of history's most terrible horrors, it is impossible to meditate about the compassion of God without asking: Where is God?

Emblazoned over the gates of the world in which we live is the escutcheon of the demons. The mark of Cain * on the face of man has come to overshadow the likeness of God. There has never been so much distress, agony and terror. It is often sinful for the sun to shine. At no time has the earth been so soaked with blood. Fellow-men have turned out to be evil spirits, monstrous and weird. Does not history look like a stage for the dance of might and evil—with man's wits too feeble to separate the two and God either directing the play or indifferent to it?

The major folly of this view seems to lie in its shifting the responsibility for man's plight from man to God, in accusing the Invisible though iniquity is ours. Rather than admit our own guilt, we seek, like Adam, to shift the blame upon someone else. For generations we have been investing life with ugliness and now we wonder why we do not succeed. God was thought of as a watchman hired to prevent us from using

* See *Genesis Rabba* 22, 12, ed. Theodor, p. 219f; L. Ginzberg, *Legends of the Jews*, vol. V, p. 141.

our loaded guns. Having failed us in this, He is now thought of as the ultimate Scapegoat.

We live in an age when most of us have ceased to be shocked by the increasing breakdown in moral inhibitions. The decay of conscience fills the air with a pungent smell. Good and evil, which were once as distinguishable as day and night, have become a blurred mist. But that mist is man-made. God is not silent. He has been silenced.

Instead of being taught to answer the direct commands of God with a conscience open to His will, men are fed on the sweetness of mythology, on promises of salvation and immortality as a dessert to the pleasant repast on earth. The faith believers cherish is second hand: it is a faith in the miracles of the past, an attachment to symbols and ceremonies. God is known from hearsay, a rumor fostered by dogmas, and even non-dogmatic thinkers offer hackneyed, solemn concepts without daring to cry out the startling vision of the sublime on the margin of which indecisions, doubts, are almost vile.

We have trifled with the name of God. We have taken ideals in vain, preached and eluded Him, praised and defied Him. Now we reap the fruits of failure. Through centuries His voice cried in the wilderness. How skilfully it was trapped and imprisoned in the temples! How thoroughly distorted! Now we behold how it gradually withdraws, abandoning one people after another, departing from their souls, despising their wisdom. The taste for goodness has all but gone from the earth.

We have witnessed in history how often a man, a group or a nation, lost from the sight of God, acts and succeeds, strives and achieves, but is given up by Him. They may stride from one victory to another and yet they are done with and abandoned, renounced and cast aside. They may possess all glory and might, but their life will be dismal. God has withdrawn from their life, even while they are heaping wickedness upon cruelty and malice upon evil. The dismissal of man, the abrogation of Providence, inaugurates eventual calamity.

They are left alone, neither molested by punishment nor assured by indication of help. The divine does not interfere with their actions nor intervene in their conscience. Having all in abundance save His blessing, they find their wealth a shell in which there is curse without mercy.

Man was the first to hide himself from God,* after having eaten of the forbidden fruit, and is still hiding.** The will of God is to be here, manifest and near; but when the doors of this world are slammed on Him, His truth betrayed, His will defied, He withdraws, leaving man to himself. God did not depart of His own volition; He was expelled. *God is in exile.*

More grave than Adam's eating the forbidden fruit was his hiding from God after he had eaten it. "Where art thou?" Where is man? is the first question that occurs in the Bible. It is man's alibi that is our problem. It is man who hides, who flees, who has an alibi. God is less rare than we think; when we long for Him, His distance crumbles away.

The prophets do not speak of the *hidden God* but of the *hiding God.* His hiding is a function not His essence, an act not a permanent state. It is when the people forsake Him, breaking the Covenant which He has made with them, that He forsakes them and hides His face from them.*** It is not

* Genesis 3:8.
** Job 13: 20–24.
*** Deuteronomy 31:16-17.

153

God who is obscure. It is man who conceals Him. His hiding from us is not in His essence: "Verily Thou art a God that hidest Thyself, O God of Israel, the Saviour!" (Isaiah 45:15). A hiding God, not a hidden God. He is waiting to be disclosed, to be admitted into our lives.

The direct effect of His hiding is the hardening of the conscience: man hears but does not understand, sees but does not perceive—his heart fat, his ears heavy.* Our task is to open our souls to Him, to let Him again enter our deeds. We have been taught the grammar of contact with God; we have been taught by the Baal Shem that His remoteness is an illusion capable of being dispelled by our faith. There are many doors through which we have to pass in order to enter the palace, and none of them is locked.

As the hiding of man is known to God and seen through, so is God's hiding seen through. In sensing the fact of His hiding we have disclosed Him. Life is a hiding place for God. We are never asunder from Him who is in need of us. Nations roam and rave—but all this is only ruffling the deep, unnoticed and uncherished stillness.

The grandchild of Rabbi Baruch was playing hide-and-seek with another boy. He hid himself and stayed in his hiding place for a long time, assuming that his friend would look for him. Finally, he went out and saw that his friend was gone, apparently not having looked for him at all, and that his own hiding had been in vain. He ran into the study of his grandfather, crying and complaining about his friend. Upon hearing the story, Rabbi Baruch broke into tears and said: "God, too, says: 'I hide, but there is no one to look for me.'"

There are times when defeat is all we face, when horror is

* Isaiah 6.

154

all that faith must bear. And yet, in spite of anguish, in spite of terror we are never overcome with ultimate dismay. "Even that it would please God to destroy me; that He would let loose His hand and cut me off, then should I yet have comfort, yea, I would exult even in my pain; let Him not spare me, for I have not denied the words of the holy One" (Job 6:9-10). Wells gush forth in the deserts of despair. This is the guidance of faith: "Lie in the dust and gorge on faith." *

We have heard with our ears, O God, our fathers have told us, what work Thou didst in their days, in the times of old.

How Thou didst drive out the heathen with Thy hand, and plantedst them; how Thou didst afflict the people, and cast them out.

For they got not the land in possession by their own sword, neither did their own arm save them: but Thy right hand, and Thine arm, and the light of Thy countenance, because Thou hadst a favour unto them.

Thou art my king, O God, command deliverances for Jacob.

Through Thee will we push down our enemies: through Thy name will we tread them under that rise up against us.

For I will not trust in my bow, neither shall my sword save me.

But Thou hast saved us from our enemies, and hast put them to shame that hated us.

In God we boast all the day long: and praise thy name for ever. Selah.

But Thou hast cast off, and put us to shame; and goest not forth with our armies.

* Rabbi Mendel of Kotzk in paraphrasing Psalm 37:3.

Thou makest us to turn back from the enemy: and they which hate us spoil for themselves.

Thou hast given us like sheep appointed for meat: and hast scattered us among the heathen.

Thou sellest thy people for nought, and dost not increase Thy wealth by their price.

Thou makest us a reproach to our neighbours, a scorn and a derision to them that are round about us.

Thou makest us a by-word among the heathen, a shaking of the head among the people.

My confusion is continually before me, and the shame of my face hath covered me:

For the voice of him that reproacheth and blasphemeth; by reason of the enemy and avenger.

All this is come upon us; yet have we not forgotten Thee: neither have we dealt falsely in Thy covenant.

Our heart is not turned back, neither have our steps declined from Thy way.

Though Thou hast sore broken us in the place of dragons, and covered us with the shadow of death.

If we have forgotten the name of our God, or stretched out our hands to a strange god:

Shall not God search this out? for He knoweth the secrets of the heart.

Yea, for Thy sake are we killed all the day long: we are counted as sheep for the slaughter.

Awake, why sleepest Thou, O Lord? arise, cast us not off for ever.

Wherefore hidest Thou Thy face? and forgettest our affliction, and our oppression?

Man is not alone

For our soul is bowed down to the dust; our belly cleaveth unto the earth.

Arise for our help, and redeem us for Thy mercies sake.

(Psalm 44)

17 Beyond Faith

To have no faith is callousness, to have undiscerning faith is superstition. "The simple believeth every word" (Proverbs 14:15),* frittering away his faith on things explorable but not yet explored. By confounding ignorance with faith he is inclined to regard as exalted whatever he fails to understand, as if faith began where understanding ended; as if it were a supreme virtue to be convinced without proofs, to be ready to believe.

Faith, the soul's urge to rise above its own wisdom, to be, like a plant, a little higher than the soil, is irrepressible, often frantic, wayward, blind and exposed to peril. The soul's affin-

---

* "To Israel, the heir of the religion of truth, the children of Jacob, the man of truth . . . it is easier to bear the burden of exile than to believe in anything before it is thoroughly and repeatedly examined and all its dross has been purged away, even though it appears to be a sign or a miracle. The undeniable evidence for Israel's love of truth and rejection of anything which is doubtful can be seen in the relation of the people of Israel to *Moses*. In spite of the fact that they were crushed by slavery, yet when Moses was told to bring them the tidings of their redemption, he said to the Lord: 'Behold, they will not believe me, nor hearken to my voice, for they will say: The Lord hath not appeared unto thee' (Exodus 4:1)" Solomon ibn Adret of Barcelona [1235–1310], Responsa no. 548.

ity for the holy is strong enough to outwit or to repress but not annihilate the force of gravitation to the vile. Those who are sure of their faith often tumble under their own weight, and, when overthrown, they fall on their knees, worshiping, deifying the snake that usually lies where flowers grow. How much tender devotion, heroism and self-mortification have been lavished upon the devil? How often has man deified Satan, found the evil magnificent though dismal, and full of indescribable majesty? Faith is, indeed, no security.

It is tragically true that we are often wrong about God, believing in that which is not God, in a counterfeit ideal, in a dream, in a cosmic force, in our own father, in our own selves. We must never cease to question our own faith and to ask what God means to us. Is He an alibi for ignorance? The white flag of surrender to the unknown? Is He a pretext for comfort and unwarranted cheer? a device to cheat despondency, fear or despair?

From whom should we seek support for our faith if even religion can be fraud, if by self-sacrifice we may hallow murder? From our minds which have so often betrayed us? From our conscience which easily fumbles and fails? From the heart? From our good intentions? "He that trusteth in his own heart is a fool" (Proverbs 28:26).

> The heart is deceitful above all things,
> It is exceedingly weak—
> Who can know it.
> (Jeremiah 17:9)

Individual faith is not self-sufficient: it must be countersigned by the dictate of unforgettable guidance.

Significantly, the Shema, the main confession of Jewish

faith, is not written in the first person and does not express a personal attitude: I believe. All it does is to recall the Voice that said: "Hear, O Israel."

TO BELIEVE IS TO REMEMBER

Not the individual man, nor a single generation by its own power, can erect the bridge that leads to God. Faith is the achievement of ages, an effort accumulated over centuries. Many of its ideas are as the light of a star that left its source centuries ago. Many songs, unfathomable today, are the resonance of voices of bygone times. There is a collective memory of God in the human spirit, and it is this memory of which we partake in our faith.

It has been suggested that the group-memory of acquired characteristics is an important factor in man's development. Some of our a priori categories are collective in character and lacking in individual content. They acquire individual character through the encounter with empirical facts. "In a sense they must be deposits from the experiences of the ancestors." *

The heritage of mankind includes not only dispositions but also ideas, "motives and images which can spring anew in every age and clime, without tradition or migration." ** "The true story of the mind is not preserved in learned volumes, but in the living mental organism of everyone." There is a treasure-house in our group memory. "Nothing has been lost except the key to this treasure-house, and even that is occasionally found."

* C. G. Jung, *Two Essays on Analytical Psychology*, London, 1928.
** C. G. Jung, *Psychological Types*, New York, 1926, p. 616.

The riches of a soul are stored up in its memory. This is the test of character—not whether a man follows the daily fashion, but whether the past is alive in his present. When we want to understand ourselves, to find out what is most precious in our lives, we search our memory. Memory is the soul's witness to the capricious mind.

Only those who are spiritually imitators, only people who are afraid to be grateful and too weak to be loyal, have nothing but the present moment. To a noble person it is a holy joy to remember, an overwhelming thrill to be grateful; while to a person whose character is neither rich nor strong, gratitude is a most painful sensation. The secret of wisdom is never to get lost in a momentary mood or passion, never to forget friendship because of a momentary grievance, never to lose sight of the lasting values because of a transitory episode. The things which sweep through our daily life should be valued according to whether or not they enrich the inner cistern. That only is valuable in our experience which is worth remembering. Remembrance is the touchstone of all actions.

Memory is a source of faith. To have faith is to remember. Jewish faith is a recollection of that which happened to Israel in the past. The events in which the spirit of God became a reality stand before our eyes painted in colors that never fade. Much of what the Bible demands can be comprised in one word: *Remember*. "Take heed to thyself, and keep thy soul diligently lest thou forget the things which thine eyes saw, and lest they depart from thy heart all the days of thy life; make them known unto thy children and thy children's children" (Deuteronomy 4:9).

Jews have not preserved the ancient monuments, they have retained the ancient moments. The light kindled in their history was never extinguished. With sustaining vitality the past survives in their thoughts, hearts, rituals. Recollection is a holy act: we sanctify the present by remembering the past.

It is perhaps for this reason that we find in some of the Jewish prayer books two summaries of the Jewish doctrine, one, based on the teaching of Maimonides, contains the famous thirteen tenets, and the other a list of remembrances.* It is as if the essential things in Judaism were not abstract ideas but rather concrete events. The exodus from Egypt, the giving of the Torah on Mount Sinai, the destruction of the Temple of Jerusalem had to be constantly present in the mind of a Jew. For over eighteen centuries the people have been away from the Holy Land, and still their attachment to the Land of Israel has never been severed. The soul of Israel has pledged: "If I forget thee, O Jerusalem, may my right hand forget its cunning" (Psalms 137:5).

Not far off from our consciousness there is a slow and silent stream, a stream not of oblivion but of memory, from which souls must constantly drink before entering the realm of faith. When drinking from that stream we do not have to take a leap in order to reach the level of faith. What we must do is to be open to the stream in order to echo, in order to recall.

There is a slow and silent stream at the shore of all of human history. The heaven is the Lord's, but the stream is open to all men. And he who lives by his faith finds himself in the community of countless men of all ages, of all nations, to whom it was shown that one man with God is a majority against all men of malice, that love of mercy is stronger than power. Creeds may divide it, zealots may deny it, the community of faith endures forever. Wars cannot destroy it, rival-

* Cf. Rabbi E. Azkari, *Haredim*, Venice, 1601, pp. 18b and 23b.

ries cannot overthrow it. If the devil offered us all the wealth of his house as a price for betraying it, he would be laughed aside.

"For from the rising of the sun even unto the going down of the same my name *is* great among the Gentiles, and in every place incense *is* offered unto my name, and a pure offering: for my name is great among the Gentiles, saith the Lord of hosts," (Malachi 1:11). This statement refers undoubtedly to the contemporaries of the prophet. But who were these worshipers of One God? At the time of Malachi there was hardly any large number of proselytes. Yet the statement declares: All those who worship their gods do not know it, but they are really worshipping Me.*

FAITH AS INDIVIDUAL MEMORY

To have faith does not mean, however, to dwell in the shadow of old ideas conceived by prophets and sages, to live off an inherited estate of doctrines and dogmas. In the realm of spirit only he who is a pioneer is able to be an heir.** The wages of

* See R. Nissim Gerondi, *Derashoth* IX, Constantinople 1530(?), p. 107a.
** The *eighteen benedictions* begin with the words: "Blessed be Thou O Lord, our God and the God of our fathers, the God of Abraham, the God of Isaac, the God of Jacob." The question has been asked: Why is it necessary to specify the three names after having said "our fathers"? That repetition, the answer goes, serves to indicate that neither Isaac nor Jacob relied entirely upon their fathers, but sought to find God themselves. This is why we speak of the God of Abraham, of Isaac, of Jacob. Rabbi Meir Eisenstadt, *Panim Me'iroth*, no. 39, Amsterdam 1715.

spiritual plagiarism is the loss of integrity; self-aggrandizement is self-betrayal.

Authentic faith is more than an echo of a tradition. It is a creative situation, an event. For God is not always silent, and man is not always blind. In every man's life there are moments when there is a lifting of the veil at the horizon of the known, opening a sight of the eternal. Each of us has at least once in his life experienced the momentous reality of God. Each of us has once caught a glimpse of the beauty, peace and power that flow through the souls of those who are devoted to Him. But such experiences or inspirations are rare events. To some people they are like shooting stars, passing and unremembered. In others they kindle a light that is never quenched. The remembrance of that experience and the loyalty to the response of that moment are the forces that sustain our faith. In this sense, *faith is faithfulness*, loyalty to an event, loyalty to our response.

FAITH AND BELIEF

A distinction is to be made between belief and mere apprehension. Not all ideas which we apprehend we accept as true. We may imagine such a thing as flying elephants but are not ready to believe in their actual existence. Belief is the mental acceptance of a proposition or a fact as true on the ground of authority or evidence; the conviction of the truth of a given proposition or an alleged fact.

Belief, in this sense, is not a theological, but an epistemological term, applying to all kinds of knowledge, and those who identify it with faith overlook the difference between the acceptance of a judgment and the acceptance of an idea of faith. Is faith only an attitude of the mind? Do we accept, in faith, the existence of God in the same way in which we accept the existence of the tower of Pisa? Faith is not the assent to an idea, but the consent to God.

Faith is a relation to God; belief a relation to an idea or a dogma. Unlike belief (which is the accompaniment of knowledge or apprehension, the assent given to what we know), faith surges beyond knowledge and apprehension; it refers not to the knowable but to that which transcends knowledge. Moreover, belief is necessarily a self-conscious act. In saying: "I believe," there is the awareness that it is the *self* that accepts something as true. Belief is *personal* conviction. Yet, in the diffidence and awe in which faith is born there is no place for self-awareness. How monstrous to think of faith as an act of man's giving his expert opinion, as an act of acknowledgment, of granting recognition to God.

A hasidic rabbi, away from home, passed the night at the house of an opponent of Hasidism. Before dawn the host, as was his custom, rose to study the Talmud. Hours passed, the rabbi stayed in bed. "How unworthy of a man reputed to be a saint to let the morning hours go by without studying the Torah." When the rabbi finally arose, the host remarked about his sleeping so late. "I have been awake for many hours," the rabbi said. "If so why did you not arise to study?" And the rabbi replied: "Before opening my eyes and praying: 'I render thanks unto Thee . . .' I began to think: Who is the 'I,' and who is the 'Thee'? How unworthy I am to render thanks unto Him. It was beyond my power to find an answer, to continue praying or to rise . . ."

Belief without faith is a formal act, often as poor in spiritual meaning as a proof for the existence of God produced by a calculating machine. Faith, on the other hand, is not only the assent to a proposition, but the staking of a whole life on the truth of an invisible reality. It is as little reducible to an assent as love, and its adequate expression is not a sober assertion but an exclamation.

FAITH AND CREED

As we have said above, we must not equate the process of faith with its expression. Accordingly, *faith*, or the act of believing, must be distinguished from *creed*, or that which we believe in. As little rational as an act of inspiration, faith becomes a dogma or a doctrine when crystallized in an opinion. In other words, what is expressed and taught as a creed is but the adaptation of the uncommon spirit to the common mind. Our creed is, like music, a translation of the unutterable into a form of expression. The original is known to God alone.

Faith is an act of spiritual audacity, while in employing terms we necessarily come to terms with our desire for intellectual security, for steadiness, tranquility.

Inaccessible to analysis are the ultimate principles of thought and action. All special sciences are compelled to take for granted a number of presuppositions that cannot be proved. These presuppositions rest either on positive intuitive certainty or are accepted for the negative reason that they are not contradicted by any experience. Nobody can explain rationally why he should sacrifice his life and happiness for the sake of the good. The conviction that we must obey ethical imperatives is not derived from logical arguments. It originates in an intuitive certitude, in a certitude of faith. On somewhat comparable fundamentals rest all positive religions. Axioms as well as dogmas can only be expressed in metaphors (the principle of the preservation of energy is a case in point), since they refer to something that surpasses experience and our means of expression are derived from experience.

The adequacy of dogmas depends upon whether they claim to formulate or to allude; in the first case they flaunt and fail, in the second they indicate and illumine. To be adequate they must retain a *telescopic* relation to the theme which they refer to; to point to the mysteries of God rather than to picture them. All they can do is to mark a way not an end of thinking. Dogmas are obstacles unless they serve as humble signposts on the way. They are allusive rather than informative or descriptive. When taken literally, they either turn flat, narrow and shallow or become ventriloquous myths. The dogma of creation, for example, has often been reduced to a tale and robbed of its authentic meaning, while as an allusion to an ultimate fact it is of inexhaustible relevance.

There are many experiences for which we have no names, many strata of faith for which we have no dogmas. Looking for a medium by which to convey the unutterable, man is too often ready to go aboard a vehicle that goes in any direction and from which it is afterwards difficult to alight.

A young man was eager to go to New York. Hitchhiking on the road, he stopped a car that was passing by: "Are you going east, to New York?"—"No, I am going west, to Chicago."—"All right, so I will go to Chicago."

Man is not alone

Man has often made a god out of a dogma, a graven image which he worshipped, to which he prayed. He would rather believe in dogmas than in God, serving them not for the sake of heaven but for the sake of a creed, the diminutive of faith.

Dogmas are the poor mind's share in the divine. A creed is almost all a poor man has. Skin for skin, he will give his life for all that he has. Yea, he may be ready to take other people's lives, if they refuse to share his tenets.

ARE DOGMAS UNNECESSARY?

Are dogmas unnecessary? We cannot be in rapport with the reality of the divine except for rare, fugitive moments. How can these moments be saved for the long hours of functional living, when the thoughts that feed like bees on the inscrutable desert us and we lose both the sight and the drive? Dogmas are like amber in which bees, once alive, are embalmed, and which are capable of being electrified when our minds become exposed to the power of the ineffable. For the problems we must always grapple with are: How to communicate those rare moments of insight to all hours of our life? How to commit intuition to concepts, the ineffable to words, communion to rational understanding? How to convey our insights to others and to unite in a fellowship of faith? It is the creed that attempts to answer these problems.*

* A discussion of these problems will be given in a sequel to this volume.

"Hear, my son, the instruction of thy father, and forsake not the teaching of thy mother" (Proverbs 1:8). Our creed is like a mother who is never impatient of our folly and failing, who does not forget, even when our faith fades into oblivion.

There are many creeds, but only one universal faith. Creeds may change, develop and wither away, while the substance of faith remains the same in all ages. The overgrowth of creed may smash and seal the doom of faith. A minimum of creed and a maximum of faith is the ideal synthesis.

FAITH AND REASON

Driven by soaring faith, leaving altitudes of wisdom behind, men of faith are occasionally overtaken by doubts: Is not faith a castle in the air in comparison with reason, which is impregnable and solid like a fortress? Men of faith are often ready to barter unexampled, inalienable insights for notions manufactured in mass production.* Yet, there is no rate of exchange for such insights, since evaluating faith in terms of reason is like trying to understand love as a syllogism and beauty as an algebraic equation.

What does our skepticism desire? To see Him on the television set? To let faith crystallize in hard currency of knowledge?

We rarely manage to erect a tower which, resting on a

* "Theologians have grown grateful for small mercies, and they do not much care what sort of God the man of science gives them so long as he gives them one at all" (B. Russell, *The Scientific Outlook,* p. 115).

170

syllogistic basis, would come up to the altitude of faith. In fact, trying to render visions of faith in terms of speculation is like constructing an airplane of massive rock.

We should not forget that in our attempts to vindicate belief, it is the creed which we examine rather than faith, the content of which is too fine to be retained in a logician's sieve.

Reason is not the measure of all things, not the all-controlling power in the life of man, not the father of all assertions. The cry of a wounded man is not the product of discursive thought. Science cannot be established in terms of art nor art in terms of science. Why, then, should faith depend for its validity upon justification by science?

The awareness of God, as we have seen, does not enter the mind by way of syllogisms nor can the certainty of faith be presented on a silver platter of speculation. Logical plausibility does not create faith nor does logical implausibility refute it.

Reason seeks to integrate the unknown with the known; faith seeks to integrate the unknown with the divine; its ripe fruit is not cold judgment but attachment, action, song and coming close to Him. While the historian explains the suffering of Israel in terms of the political geography of Palestine, which, situated astride the crossroads of three continents, was exposed to the ambitions of conquerors, the prophet speaks of a divine plan to let Israel be afflicted in order to atone, not for its own sins, but also for the sins of the heathen.

When transformed into creed, faith is rendered in conventional terms of reason. Such terms come and go, and what is lucid today may be a travesty tomorrow. Reason's great conflict is not with faith but with belief.

171

"No greater evil can happen to anyone than to hate reasoning. But hatred of reasoning and hatred of mankind both spring from the same source . . . Pay little attention to Socrates, but much more to the truth; and if I appear to you to say anything true, assent to it; but if not, oppose me with all your might" (*Phaedo* 87.91).

In Jewish tradition reason has always been esteemed as one of God's foremost gifts to man. It would be hard to discover in the history of Jewish thought a tendency to conspire against or to defy its conclusions. The first thing the Jews pray for, three times a day, is not daily bread, health or even forgiveness of sins, but knowledge: "O grant us knowledge, understanding, insight."

If the only safety of a creed lay in its being entrenched behind the wall of stubborn believing, then behind it would be fear, not faith; misgiving, not trust. Truth has nothing to fear from reason. What we abhor is presumptuousness that often goes with super-rationalism, reason conditioned by conceit, reason subservient to passion.

That there can be no true conflict between the teachings imparted to us by revelation and the ideas acquired by reason was a prevalent opinion of the great Jewish thinkers of the Middle Ages. The idea of their intrinsic agreement was, to the mind of these thinkers, a necessary implication of the doctrine of monotheism. What is contained in the divine message can neither misrepresent reality nor contradict any truths taught by science, since both reason and revelation originated in the wisdom of God who created all reality and knows all truth. An essential disagreement between reason and revelation would presuppose the existence of two divine beings, each of whom would represent a different source of knowledge. Faith, therefore, can never compel the reason to accept that which is absurd.

Neither reason nor faith is all-inclusive nor self-sufficient. The insights of faith are general, vague and stand in need of conceptualization in order to be communicated to the mind, integrated and brought to consistency. Reason is a necessary coefficient of faith, lending form to what often becomes violent, blind and exaggerated by imagination. *Faith without reason is mute; reason without faith is deaf.*

But do we really believe? A Hasid once started to recite the thirteen principles of Maimonides: "I firmly believe that the Creator, blessed be His name, is the Creator and Ruler of all created beings" . . . Suddenly he paused: "Can I say that I firmly believe? If I did, I would not be so fretful, so profane; I would not pray so half-heartedly . . . But if I do not, how dare I tell a lie . . . No, I will not say it; a liar is worse than a non-believer . . . Yet, this would mean, I do not believe. But I do believe! . . ." Again he paused, until he found a way out. He decided to say: "Oh that I might firmly believe . . ."

Ezra the Scribe, the great renovator of Judaism, of whom the rabbis said that he was worthy of receiving the Torah, had it not been already given through Moses (Sanhedrin 21b), confessed his lack of perfect faith. He tells us that after he had received a royal firman from King Artaxerxes granting him permission to lead a group of exiles from Babylonia: "I proclaimed a fast there at the river Ahava, that we might afflict ourselves before our God, to seek of Him a right way for us, and for our little ones, and for all our substance. For I was ashamed to require of the King a band of soldiers and horsemen to help us against the enemy in the way: because we had spoken unto the king, saying, the hand of God is upon all them for good that seek Him" (Ezra 8:21-22).

For faith is not the clinging to a shrine but an endless pilgrimage of the heart. Audacious longing, burning songs, daring thoughts, an impulse overwhelming the heart, usurping the mind—these are all a drive towards serving Him who rings our hearts like a bell. It is as if He were waiting to enter our empty, perishing lives.

To rely on our faith would be idol-worship. We have only the right to rely on God. Faith is not an insurance, but a constant effort, constant listening to the eternal voice.

Accordingly, faith is not a feature of man's mentality: self-effacement of curiosity, asceticism of reason, some psychic quality that has bearing on man alone. Its essence is not disclosed in the way we utter it, but in the soul's being in accord with what is relevant to God; in the extension of our love to what God may approve, our being carried away by the tide of His thoughts, rising beyond the desolate ken of man's despair. Faith is real only when it is not one-sided but reciprocal. Man can rely on God, if God can rely on man. We may trust in Him because He trusts in us.* To have faith means to justify God's faith in man. It is as essential that God believe in man

* Faith is ascribed to God in Deuteronomy 32:4.

174

as that man should believe in God. Thus faith is awareness of divine mutuality and companionship, a form of communion between God and man.

RELIGION IS MORE THAN INWARDNESS

We are often inclined to define the essence of religion as a state of the soul, as inwardness, as an absolute feeling, and expect a person who is religious to be endowed with a kind of sentiment too deep to rise to the surface of common deeds, as if religion were a plant that can only thrive at the bottom of the ocean. As we have seen, religion is not a feeling for something that is, but an answer to Him who is asking us to live in a certain way. It is in its very origin a consciousness of duty, of being committed to higher ends; a realization that life is not only man's but also God's sphere of interest.

Faith does not come to an end with attaining certainty of His existence. Faith is the beginning of intense craving to enter a synthesis with Him who is beyond the mystery, to bring together all the might that is within us with all that is spiritual beyond us. At the root of our yearning for integrity is a stir of the inexpressible within us to commune with the ineffable beyond us. But what is the language of that communion, without which our impulse remains inarticulate?

We are taught that what God asks of man is more than an inner attitude, that He gives man not only life but also a law, that His will is to be served not only adored, obeyed not only worshipped. Faith comes over us like a force urging for action, to which we respond by pledging ourselves to constancy of devotion, committing us to the presence of God, and remains an affiliation for life, an allegiance involving restraint, submission, self-control and courage.

Judaism insists upon establishing a unity of faith and creed, of piety and Halacha, of devotion and deed. Faith is but a seed, while the deed is its growth or decay. Faith disembodied, faith that tries to grow in splendid isolation, is but a ghost, for which there is no place in our psycho-physical world.

What *creed* is in relation to *faith*, the *Halacha* is in relation to *piety*. As faith cannot exist without a creed, piety cannot subsist without a pattern of deeds; as intelligence cannot be separated from training, religion cannot be divorced from conduct. Judaism is lived in deeds not only in thoughts.

A pattern for living—the object of man's most urgent quest— which would correspond to his dignity, must take into consideration not only his ability to exploit the forces of nature and to appreciate the loveliness of its forms, but also his unique sense of the ineffable. It must be a design, not only for the satisfaction of needs, but also for the attainment of ends.

II. THE PROBLEM OF LIVING

18 The Problem of Needs

While man is attached to the ultimate at the root of his being, he is detached and uncurbed in his thoughts and deeds, free to act and free to refrain; he has the power to disobey. Yet a tree is known by its fruits, not by its roots. There are no ugly trees but there are wormy fruits. Only one question, therefore, is worthy of supreme anxiety: How to live in a world pestered with lies and remain unpolluted, how not to be stricken with despair, not to flee but to fight and succeed in keeping the soul unsoiled and even aid in purifying the world?

Such strength, such guidance cannot be wrested from the stars. Nature is too aloof or too old to teach confused man how to discern right and wrong. The sense of the ineffable is necessary, but not sufficient to find the way from wonder to worship, from willingness to realization, from awe to action.

Western philosophy has suffered its tragic defeat as a consequence of the fondness of its great masters for the problem of cognition. Guided by the assumption that he who knows how to think will know how to live, philosophy has, since the days of Socrates, been primarily a quest of right thinking. Particularly since the time of Descartes, it concentrated its attention on the problem of cognition, becoming less and less aware of the problem of living. In fact, the less relevant to living a problem was, the more respectable and worthy of exploration it appeared to philosophers.

However, thinking about ultimate problems is more than a particular skill. It is an act of the total personality,* a process which all faculties of mind and soul are thrown in, and is necessarily affected by the personal climate in which it comes to pass; we think the way we live. To think what we sense, we must live what we think. If culture is to be more than the product of a hothouse, then it must grow out of the soil of daily living, and in turn affect the inner stronghold of the human personality. Culture has to grow from within outward, from the concrete existence, conduct and condition of man.

THE PROBLEM OF THE NEUTRAL

The problem of living does not arise with the question of how to take care of the rascals or with the realization of how we blunder in dealing with other people. It begins in the relation to our own selves, in the handling of our physiological and emotional functions. What is first at stake in the life of man is not the fact of sin, of the wrong and corrupt, but the natural acts, the *needs*. Our possessions pose no less a problem than our passions. The primary task, therefore, is not how to deal with

* Compare Chapter 8.

the *evil*, but how to deal with the *neutral*, how to deal with needs.

The will would remain dormant in human nature if not for the fact that there is a way in which it is constantly aroused. The way is the *experience of needs*, the feeling of pressure and urgency arising from internal or external causes, for the satisfaction of which man must bring his latent forces into action.

Needs, then, are man's system of communication with his inside and outside world. They report to the consciousness the necessities of living, but they also determine the aims he selects for planning and action. Things in the world around him often, though not always, remain outside his ken, until they become objects of his needs.

Engrossed in his thoughts and feelings, man may shut himself out of his environment, and it is his needs in which he meets the world again. They are the crossroads of internal and external life. It is, therefore, through an analysis of needs that we should approach the problem of living.

Specifically, need denotes the absence or shortage of something indispensable to the well-being of a person, evoking the urgent desire for satisfaction.* Psychologically, wherever

* The term "need" is generally used in two ways: one denoting the actual lack, an objective condition, and the other denoting the awareness of such a lack. It is in the second sense, in which need is synonymous with interest, namely "an unsatisfied capacity corresponding to an unrealized condition" that the term is used here.

there is a need, there is a desire to satisfy the need, and where a desire is not felt, the need has not been expressed. *Ignoti nulla cupido.* "There is no desire for what is unknown" (Ovid *Ars Amatoria*, iii.1.397). We yearn only for that of which we know.

> The jewel that we find we stoop and take't
> Because we see it; but what we do not see
> We tread upon, and never think of it.
> (Shakespeare, *Measure for Measure*, Act II, Scene 1)

LIFE—A CLUSTER OF NEEDS

Every human being is a cluster of needs, yet these needs are not the same in all men nor unalterable in any one man. There is a fixed minimum of needs for all men, but no fixed maximum for any man. Unlike animals, man is the playground for the unpredictable emergence and multiplication of needs and interests, some of which are indigenous to his nature, while others are induced by advertisement, fashion, envy, or come about as miscarriages of authentic needs. We usually fail to discern between authentic and artificial needs and, misjudging a whim for an aspiration, we are thrown into ugly tensions. Most obsessions are the perpetuation of such misjudgments. In fact, more people die in the epidemics of needs than in the epidemics of disease.

If man's biological evolution may be explained as adaptation to his environment, the advancement of civilization must be defined as the adjustment of environmental conditions to human needs. There are no material wants that science and technology do not promise to supply. To stem the expansion of man's needs which in turn is brought about by technological and social advancement, would mean to halt the stream on which civilization is riding. Yet the stream unchecked may sweep away civilization itself, since the pressure of needs turned into aggressive interests is the constant cause of wars and increases in direct proportion to technological progress. Morality, trying to sit in judgment and to distinguish between just and unjust interests, appears too late on the stage to be effective. When interests have become entrenched, no maxims can drive them away. The soul is slippery, filled with a mob of desires and resentments, unruly, fickle and loath to accept the hegemony of reason.

THE INADEQUACY OF ETHICS

The most pressing and most ignored of problems—how to live—will not be solved through teaching sagacious rules. Knowledge of ethics is as far from being identical with virtue as erudition in musical theory is from making one an artist. One may be learned and wicked, an authority on ethical theory and a scoundrel, know how to condemn anger and be unable to curb it. Life is not lived in the form of a debate among member faculties of the soul, in which the most persuasive wins the argument. Life is often war, in which disorderly forces of folly, fancy and passion are thrown into battle, a war which cannot be won by the noble magic of merely remembering a golden rule. How should a wise abstraction be expected to compete with rage, cunning, insatiability and favoritism of the ego to itself?

It is true that our reason is responsive to reasonable arguments. Yet, reason is a lonely stranger in the soul, while the irrational forces feel at home and are always in the majority. Why bear hardship on behalf of virtue? Why act against nature and choose the right when pleasure abounds on the side of vice? Why forego that which one naturally should prefer or voluntarily endure that which one naturally should avoid?

Ethics expects man to consult his power of judgment, decide what action to take in the light of general principles and faithfully carry out the wise decision. Thus, it not only underestimates the difficulty in applying general rules to particular situations, which are often intricate, perplexing and ambivalent, but also expects every man to combine within himself judicial and executive powers. Moreover, while telling us what we are fighting for, ethical theory fails to tell us how to win the struggle; while telling us that we ought to, it does not tell us how to achieve mastery over folly and madness. It is true that ethics demands the acquisition of good habits, not only learning. However, no amount of habits can embrace the totality of living.

THE PERIL OF LIVING

Grave emergencies we mostly meet unprepared, in spite of our education that aims to prepare us for challenges to come. No one is able to rive the future and to see the exigencies it holds in store for him. No one can calculate the coils and whorls in which the spiral nebula of life will turn, or predict to what depth envy, passion and desire for prestige may carry a person. What should we do beforehand to ward off a sudden subconscious urge to avenge, to insult, to hurt? A single vicious thought may spread like canker at the roots of all other thoughts, and one person with evil becomes quickly a majority against a multitude of people impartial to evil. Man is not made for neutrality, for being aloof or indifferent, nor can the world remain a vacuum; unless we make it an altar to God, it is invaded by demons.

With a capacity to hurt boundless and unchecked, with the immense expansion of power and the rapid decay of compassion, life has, indeed, become a synonym for peril. Upon whom shall we rely for protection against our own selves? How shall we replenish the tiny stream of integrity in our souls? Countless are the situations in which we witness how the power of judgment wanes in vagrant minds, how integrity collides with a contemptible desire that comes out of the way.

> O, what men dare do! What men may do!
> What men daily do, not knowing what they do.
> (Shakespeare, *Much Ado About Nothing*,
> Act IV, Scene 1, 1.19)

One of the lessons we have derived from the events of our time is that we cannot dwell at ease under the sun of civilization, that man is the least harmless of beings. It is as if every minute were packed with tension like the interlude between lightning and thunder, and our moral order were a display of ancient oaks with ephemeral roots. It took one storm to turn a civilization into an inconceivable inferno.

Trees do not die of age, but because of barriers that prevent the rays of the sun from reaching them, because of branches that lose self-restraint, spreading more than the roots can stand. We today may rarely gaze at the sky or horizon, yet there are lightnings that even overbearing trees do not cease to dread. Only fools are afraid to fear and to listen to the constant collapse of task and time over their heads, with life being buried beneath the ruins.

NEEDS ARE NOT HOLY

Needs are looked upon today as if they were holy, as if they contained the quintessence of eternity. Needs are our gods, and we toil and spare no effort to gratify them. Suppression of a desire is considered a sacrilege that must inevitably avenge itself in the form of some mental disorder. We worship not one but a whole pantheon of needs and have come to look upon moral and spiritual norms as nothing but personal desires in disguise.

It is, indeed, grotesque that while in science the *anthropocentric* view of the earth as the center of the universe and of man as the purpose of all being has long been discarded, in actual living an *egocentric* view of man and his needs as the measure of all values, with nothing to determine his way of living except his own needs, continues to be cherished. If satisfaction of human desires were taken as the measure of all things, then the world, which never squares with our needs, would have to be considered an abysmal failure. Human nature is insatiable and achievements never keep pace with evolving needs.

Man is not alone

We cannot make our judgments, decisions and directions for actions dependent upon our needs. The fact is that man who has found out so much about so many things knows neither his own heart nor his own voice. Many of the interests and needs we cherish are imposed on us by the conventions of society rather than being indigenous to our essence. While some of them are necessities, others, as noted above, are fictitious, and adopted as a result of convention, advertisement or sheer envy.

The modern mind believes that it possesses the philosopher's stone in the concept of needs. But who knows his true needs? How are we going to discern authentic from fictitious needs, necessities from make-believes?

As a rule, we become aware of our authentic craving suddenly, unexpectedly; not at the beginning of, but late in the course of our careers. Since we rarely understand what we want until it is almost too late, our feeling cannot be an index of what is essential. We are all eager and ready to subdue the inimical forces of nature, to fight what is hostile to our physical survival, disease, enemies, danger. But how many of us are eager and ready to subdue the evil within us or to fight crime when it does not threaten our own survival, the decay of soul, the enemy within our needs?

Having absorbed an enormous amount of needs and having been taught to cherish the high values, such as justice, liberty, faith, as private interests, we are beginning to wonder whether needs and interests should be relied upon. While it is true that there are interests which all men have in common, most of our private interests, as asserted in daily living, divide and antagonize rather than unite us.

Interest is a subjective, dividing principle. It is the excitement of feeling, accompanying special attention paid to some object. But do we pay sufficient attention to the demands for universal justice? In fact, the interest in universal welfare is usually blocked by the interest in personal welfare, particularly when it is to be achieved at the price of renouncing one's personal interests. It is just because the power of interests is tyrannizing our lives, determining our views and actions, that we lose sight of the values that count most.

RIGHT AND WRONG NEEDS

Short is the way from need to greed. Evil conditions make us seethe with evil needs, with mad dreams. Can we afford to pursue all our innate needs, even our will for power?

In the tragic confusion of interests, in which every one of us is caught, no distinction seems to be as indispensable as the distinction between right and wrong interests. Yet the concepts of right and wrong, to be standards in our dealing with interests, cannot themselves be interests. Determined as they are by temperament, bias, background and environment of every individual and group, needs are our problems rather than our norms. They are in need of, rather than the origins of standards.

How could individual or national eagerness be the measure of what is objectively required, if whole nations may be persuaded to cherish evil interests? If a universal state should ever be established and mankind by a majority of votes should decide that a particular ethnic group is to be exterminated, because this would suit the interests of mankind, would that decision be right? Or would the statement of a creditor nation that $2 + 2 = 5$ be correct? An action is right, a statement is true, regardless of whether it is expedient or not.

The true is not what is opportune, nor is that which we desire for the satisfaction of urgent needs necessarily right. What is right may correspond to our present interest, but our interest in itself is not right. Right is beyond the feeling of interest. It may demand doing things which we do not feel the need of, things required but not desired.

He who sets out to employ the realities of life as means for satisfying his own desires will soon forfeit his freedom and be degraded to a mere tool. Acquiring things, he becomes enslaved to them; in subduing others, he loses his own soul. It is as if unchecked covetousness were double-faced; a sneer and subtle vengeance behind a captivating smile. We can ill afford to set up needs, an unknown, variable, vacillating and eventually degrading factor, as a universal standard, as a supreme, abiding rule or pattern for living.

We feel jailed in the confinement of personal needs. The more we indulge in satisfactions, the deeper is our feeling of oppressiveness. To be an iconoclast of idolized needs, to defy our own immoral interests, though they seem to be vital and have long been cherished, we must be able to say *no* to ourselves in the name of a higher *yes*. Yet our minds are late, slow and erratic. What can give us the power to curb the deference to wrong needs, to detect spiritual fallacies, to ward off false ideals and to wrestle with inattentiveness to the unseemly and holy?

Needs cannot be dealt with one by one but only all at once, at their root. To understand the problem of needs, we must face the problem of man, the subject of needs. Man is animated by more needs than any other being.* They seem to lie beneath his will and are independent of his volition. They are the source rather than the product of desire. Consequently, we shall only be able to judge needs if we succeed in understanding the meaning of existence.

* See p. 138.

19 The Meaning of Existence

Our theories will go awry, will all throw dust into our eyes, unless we dare to confront not only the world but the soul as well, and begin to be amazed at our lack of amazement in being alive, at our taking life for granted.

Confronting the soul is an intellectual exposure that tears open the mind to incalculable questions, the answers to which are not easily earned. Modern man, therefore, believes that his security lies in refraining from raising such issues. Ultimate questions have become the object of his favorite unawareness. Since the dedication to tangible matters is highly rewarded, he does not care to pay attention to imponderable issues and prefers to erect a tower of Babel on the narrow basis of deeper unawareness.

Unawareness of the ultimate is a possible state of mind as long as man finds tranquility in his dedication to partial objectives. But when the tower begins to totter, when death wipes away that which seemed mighty and independent, when in evil days the delights of striving are replaced by the nightmare of futility, he becomes conscious of the peril of evasive-ness, of the emptiness of small objectives. His apprehension lest in winning small prizes he did not gamble his life away, throws his soul open to questions he was trying to avoid.

THE MEANING OF EXISTENCE

But what is there at stake in human life that may be gambled away? It is the meaning of life. In all acts he performs, man raises a claim to meaning. The trees he plants, the tools he invents, are *answers to a need* or a purpose. In its very essence, consciousness is a dedication to design. Committed to the task of coalescing being with meaning, things with ideas, the mind is driven to ponder whether meaning is something it may invent and invest, something which ought to be attained, or whether there is meaning to existence as it is, to existence as existence, independent of what we may add to it. In other words, is there only meaning to what *man does*, but none to what *he is*? Becoming conscious of himself he does not stop at knowing: "I am"; he is driven to know "what" he is. Man may, indeed, be characterized as *a subject in quest of a predicate*, as a being in quest of a meaning of life, of all of life, not only of particular actions or single episodes which happen now and then.

Meaning denotes a condition that cannot be reduced to a material relation and grasped by the sense organs. Meaning is compatibility with an idea, it is, furthermore, that which a fact is for the sake of something else; the pregnancy of an object with value. Life is precious to man. But is it precious to him alone? Or is someone else in need of it?

192

Man is not alone

Imbedded in the mind is a certainty that the state of existence and the state of meaning stand in a relation to each other, that life is assessable in terms of meaning. The will to meaning and the certainty of the legitimacy of our striving to ascertain it are as intrinsically human as the will to live and the certainty of being alive.

In spite of failures and frustrations, we continue to be haunted by that irrepressible quest. We can never accept the idea that life is hollow and incompatible with meaning.

If at the root of philosophy is not a self-contempt of the mind but the mind's concern for its ultimate surmise, then our aim is to examine in order to know. Seeking contentment in a brilliant subterfuge, we are often ready to embezzle the original surmise. But why should we even care to doubt, if we cease to surmise? Philosophy is what man dares to do with his ultimate surmise of meaning in existence.

Animals are content when their needs are satisfied; man insists not only on being satisfied but also on being able to satisfy, on *being a need* not only on *having needs*. Personal needs come and go, but one anxiety remains: *Am I needed?* There is no man who has not been moved by that anxiety.

It is a most significant fact that man is not sufficient to himself, that life is not meaningful to him unless it is serving an end beyond itself, unless it is of value to someone else. The self may have the highest rate of exchange, yet men do not live by currency alone, but by the good attainable in expending it. To hoard the self is to grow a colossal sense for the futility of living.

Man is not an all-inclusive end to himself. The second maxim of Kant, never to use human beings merely as means but to regard them also as ends, only suggests how a person ought to be treated by other people, not how he ought to treat himself. For if a person thinks that he is an end to himself, then he will use others as means. Moreover, if the idea of man being an end is to be taken as a true estimate of his worth, he cannot be expected to sacrifice his life or his interests for the good of someone else or even of a group. He must treat himself the way he expects others to treat him. Why should even a group or a whole people be worth the sacrifice of one's life? To a person who regards himself as an absolute end a thousand lives will not be worth more than his own life.

Sophisticated thinking may enable man to feign his being sufficient to himself. Yet the way to insanity is paved with such illusions. The feeling of futility that comes with the sense of being useless, of not being needed in the world, is the most common cause of psychoneurosis. The only way to avoid despair is *to be a need* rather than an end. *Happiness*, in fact, may be defined as the *certainty of being needed*. But *who is* in need of man?

DOES MAN EXIST FOR THE SAKE OF SOCIETY?

The first answer that comes to mind is a social one—man's purpose is to serve society or mankind. The ultimate worth of a person would then be determined by his usefulness to others, by the efficiency of his social work. Yet, in spite of his instrumentalist attitude, man expects others to take him not for what he may mean to them but as a being valuable in himself. Even he who does not regard himself as an absolute end, rebels against being treated as a means to an end, as subservient to other men. The rich, the men of the world, want to be loved for their own sake, for their essence, whatever it may mean, not for their achievements or possessions. Nor do the old and sick expect help because of what they may give us in return. Who needs the old, the incurably sick, the maintenance of whom is a drain on the treasury of the state? It is, moreover, obvious that such service does not claim all of one's life and can therefore not be the ultimate answer to his quest of meaning for life as a whole. Man has more to give than what other men are able or willing to accept. To say that life could consist of care for others of incessant service to the world, would be a vulgar boast. What we are able to bestow upon others is usually less and rarely more than a tithe.

There are alleys in the soul where man walks alone, ways that do not lead to society, a world of privacy that shrinks from the public eye. Life comprises not only arable, productive land, but also mountains of dreams, an underground of sorrow, towers of yearning, which can hardly be utilized to the last for the good of society, unless man be converted into a machine in which every screw must serve a function or be removed. It is a profiteering state which, trying to exploit the individual, asks all of man for itself.

And if society as embodied in the state should prove to be corrupt and my effort to cure its evil unavailing, would my life as an individual have been totally void of meaning? If society should decide to reject my services and even place me in solitary confinement, so that I will surely die without being able to bequeath any influence to the world I love, will I then feel compelled to end my life?

Human existence cannot derive its ultimate meaning from society, because society itself is in need of meaning. It is as legitimate to ask: Is mankind needed?—as it is to ask: Am I needed?

Humanity begins in the individual man, just as history takes its rise from a singular event. It is always one man at a time whom we keep in mind when we pledge: "with malice toward none, with charity for all," or when trying to fulfill: "Love thy neighbor as thyself." The term "mankind," which in biology denotes the human species, has an entirely different meaning in the realm of ethics and religion. Here mankind is not conceived as a species, as an abstract concept, stripped from its concrete reality, but as an abundance of specific individuals; as a community of persons rather than as a herd or a multitude of nondescripts.

While it is true that the good of all counts more than the good of one, it is the concrete individual who lends meaning to the human race. We do not think that a human being is valuable because he is a member of the race; it is rather the opposite: the human race is valuable because it is composed of human beings.

While dependent on society as well as on the air that sustains us, and while other men compose the system of relations in which the curve of our actions takes its course, it is as individuals that we are beset with desires, fears and hopes, challenged, called upon and endowed with the power of will and a spark of responsibility.

THE SELF-ANNIHILATION OF DESIRE

Of all phenomena which take place in the soul, desires have the highest rate of mortality. Like aquatic plants, they grow and live in the waters of oblivion, impatiently eager to vanish. Inherent in desire is the intention to expire; it asserts itself in order to be quenched, and in attaining satisfaction it comes to an end, singing its own dirge.

Such suicidal intention is not vested in all human acts. Thoughts, concepts, laws, theories are born with the intent to endure. A problem, for example, does not cease to be relevant when its solution is achieved. Inherent in reason is the intention to endure, a striving to comprehend the valid, to form concepts the cogency of which goes on for ever. It is, therefore, not in pondering about ideas, but in surveying one's inner life and discovering the graveyard of needs and desires, once fervently cherished, that we become intimately aware of the temporality of existence.

197

Yet, there is a curious ambiguity in the way in which this awareness is entertained. For while there is nothing man is more intimately sure of than the temporality of existence, he is rarely
resigned to the role of a mere undertaker of desires.

Walking upon a rock that is constantly crumbling away behind every step and anticipating the inevitable abruption which
will end his walk, man cannot restrain his bitter yearning to
know whether life is nothing but a series of momentary physiological and mental processes, actions and forms of behavior, a
flow of vicissitudes, desires and sensations, running like grains
through an hourglass, marking time only once and always vanishing.

He wonders whether, at the bottom, life is not like the face
of the sundial, outliving all shadows that rotate upon its surface. Is life nothing but a medley of facts, unrelated to one
another; chaos camouflaged by illusion?

THE HELPLESS CRAVING

There is not a soul on this earth which, however vaguely or
rarely, has not realized that life is dismal if not mirrored in
something which is lasting. We are all in search of a conviction that there is something which is worth the toil of living.
There is not a soul which has not felt a craving to know of
something that outlasts life, strife and agony.

Man is not alone

Helpless and incongruous is man with all his craving, with his tiny candles in the mist. Is it his will to be good that would heal the wounds of his soul, his fright and frustration? It is too obvious that his will is a door to a house divided against itself, that his good intentions, after enduring for a while, touch the mud of vanity, like the horizon of his life which some day will touch the grave. Is there anything beyond the horizon of our good intentions?

Man's quest for a meaning of existence is essentially a quest for the lasting, a quest for abidingness. In a sense, human life is often a race against time, going through efforts to perpetuate experiences, attaching itself to values or establishing relations that do not perish at once. His quest is not a product of desire but an essential element of his nature, characteristic not only of his mind but also of his very existence. This can be shown by analyzing the structure of existence as such.

WHAT IS EXISTENCE?

While existence as a general category remains indefinable, it is directly known to us and, in spite of its indefinability, not entirely out of relation to the mind. It is not an empty concept, since even as a most general category it cannot be completely divested of some relations. There is always a minimum of meaning in our notion of existence.

The most intrinsic characteristic of existence is independence. What exists does so in reality, in time and space, not only in our minds. In ascribing existence to a person, we imply that the person is more than a mere word, name or idea, that he exists independent of us and our thinking, while that which is a product of our imagination, like the chimerical Brobdingnags or the Yahoos, depends entirely on our mind; it is non-existent when we do not think of it. However, existence thus described is a negative concept which tells us what existence is not and places it out of relation to us. But what is the positive content of existence? Does not existence imply a necessary relation to something beyond itself?

THE TEMPORALITY OF EXISTENCE

It is obvious that the relation of existence to time is more intimate and unique than its relation to space. There is nothing in space which is so necessary to existence, or belongs so intimately to it, that we could not abandon it without incurring any radical harm. Existence implies no possession of property, no mastery over other beings. Even the particular position we occupy in space we can freely exchange for another one, while the years of our lives are of absolute importance to us. Time is the only property the self really *owns*. Temporality, therefore, is an essential feature of existence.

Time, however, is the most flimsy of things: a mere succession of perishing instants. It is something we never hold: the past is gone forever, what is yet to come is beyond our reach, and the present departs before we can perceive it. How paradoxical and true—the only property we own we never possess.

Man is not alone

The temporality or evanescence of existence is, indeed, painfully obvious to all of us. Caught in the mortal stream of time, which permits us neither to abide in the present nor to return to any moment of the past, the only prospect we constantly face is that of ceasing to exist, of being thrown out of the stream. Yet, is it temporality alone that is intrinsic to existence? Is not permanence, to some degree, just as intrinsic to it? Existence implies duration, continuity. Existence is *uninterruptedness*, not a year now and a year then, dispersion, but continuous extension. Relative and limited as life's uninterruptedness may be, it is, like temporality, one of the two constitutive characteristics of existence.

There is an element of constancy in the inner structure of existence which accounts for permanence within temporality, as it is the enduring aspect of reality which alone is capable of being an object of logical judgment. For only that aspect of a thing which is constant and which remains the same, independent of the changes which the thing itself undergoes, can be grasped by the categories of our reason. In other words, our categories are the mirrors, in which the things are reflected in the light of their constancy. There is nothing which the mind esteems more than abidingness. We measure values by their endurance.

Even our consciousness of time depends upon a principle that is independent of time. We are conscious of time by measuring it, by saying a minute, an hour, a day. Yet in order to measure time, we must be in possession of a principle of measurement which is taken to be constant. We cannot measure it by directly comparing one stretch of time with another, for two parts of time are never given at once. Thus, time itself cannot yield a consciousness of itself, for in order to be a consciousness of itself it would have to be equally present at all stages of time. Consciousness of time, therefore, presupposes a principle that is not temporal and does not, like each instant, vanish to give birth to the next one. Time itself depends for its continuation on a principle that is independent of time, for time itself could not yield permanence. The stream of time flows along a "no time's land."

THE SECRET OF EXISTENCE

It is in this relation of temporality to abidingness that the secret of existence resides. For whether we attempt to explain, for example, organic living by postulating a mysterious "vital force" or by physico-chemical laws exclusively, the basic question remains unanswered: What makes that force or those laws endure? Is the driving force of living the will to live? But the will itself is subject to change. Obviously, there must be some permanent principle that gives duration to the will. If so, what is the relation of the will to live to that principle? Moreover, is it true that existence is the result of a deliberate decision? Does my organism grow, multiply and develop because it wants to? Are the urge, endeavor, daring and adventure which characterize life the result of choice? If so, we are not aware of it. We know, on the contrary, that human will never creates life. In generating life, we are the tools not the masters. We are witnesses rather than authors of birth and death. We know that something animates and inspires a living organism. But what? To use the concept of a subconscious will to live, of a will that we do not know ourselves, is like employing a *deus ex machina*, the device whereby in ancient drama a god was brought to the stage to provide a supernatural solution to a dramatic difficulty, with the difference, however, that here the *deus* appears in disguise, claiming to be a natural being.

What is the lasting in our own lives? What remains constant through all changes? The body grows and decays; the passions all flow down the stream of oblivion. What does a man, looking back on the threshold of death, consider *lasting* in all that has happened and passed? Is it our will to live? Our reflective concern?

IN BEING WE OBEY

Looking at our own existence, we are forced to admit that the essence of existence is not in our will to live; we must live, and in living we obey. Existence is a compliance, not a desire; an agreement, not an impulse. *In being we obey.*

We struggle, suffer, live and act, not because we have the will to. Our will itself is obedience, an answer, a compliance. It is only subsequently that we get to *will* what we *must;* the will is appearance, our compliance—"the thing in itself." Is not the life of the body a process of obedience. What is thinking, if not submission to truth, compliance with the rules of logic? For the fact that there is logic, independent of wishful thinking, exercising over our minds coercive, implacable power is unexplainable as a product of the will or mind. The acts of logical thinking are the mind's, but that there must be logic at all, that the mind cannot but think in accordance to its rules, is *not* the mind's.

We have characterized man's quest for a meaning of existence as a quest for the lasting, and have shown that the relation to the lasting is at the root of all existence. Yet the natural piety of obedience is no answer to man's quest. For while man is attached to the lasting at the root of his being, he is, as we stated above, detached and uncurbed in his thoughts and deeds; he is free to act and free to refrain; he has the power to disobey. It is because of his being independent that he is haunted by a fear of his life being irrelevant and by a will to ultimate meaning.

Every human being harbors a craving for the lasting, yet few of us comprehend the meaning of the lasting. There is only one truth but there are many ways of misunderstanding it. There is only one goal, but there are many ways of missing it.

What is the ultimate goal? The prolongation of existence in its present form with its pleasures and cares? The perpetuation of the self with its languor, vanity and fear? We do not love the totality of the ego to such a degree that our highest aspiration should be to preserve it forever. In fact, we begin to brood about immortality in our anxiety about the perpetuation of others rather than in an anxiety about the perpetuation of our own selves. The thought of immortality begins in compassion, in a transitive concern for those who have been taken away.

204

Man is not alone

The true aspiration is not that self and all that is contained in it may last, but that all the self stands for may last. Man can be a nightmare but also a fulfilment of a vision of God. He has been given the power to surpass himself; to answer for all things and to act for one God. All beings obey the law; man is able to sing the law. His ultimate legacy is in his composing a song of deeds which only God fully understands.

TIME AND ETERNITY

The way to the lasting does not lie on the other side of life; it does not begin where time breaks off. The lasting begins not beyond but *within time*, within the moment, within the concrete. Time can be seen from two aspects: from the aspect of *temporality* and from the aspect of *eternity*.

Time is the border of eternity. Time is eternity formed into tassels. The moments of our lives are like luxuriant tassels. They are attached to the garment and are made of the same cloth. It is through spiritual living that we realize that the infinite can be confined in a measured line.

Life without integrity is like loosely hanging threads, easily straying from the main cloth, while in acts of piety we learn to understand that every instant is like a thread raveling out of eternity to form a delicate tassel. We must not cast off the threads but weave them into the design of an eternal fabric.

The days of our lives are representatives of eternity rather than fugitives, and we must live as if the fate of all of time would totally depend on a single moment.

Seen as temporality, the essence of time is detachment, isolation. A temporal moment is always alone, always exclusive. Two instants can never be together, never contemporary. Seen as eternity, the essence of time is attachment, communion. It is within time rather than within space that we are able to commune, to worship, to love. It is within time that one day may be worth a thousand years.

Creative insights grow a life-time to last a moment, and yet they last for ever. For to last means to commune with God, "to cleave unto Him" (Deuteronomy 11:22). A moment has no contemporary within temporality. But within eternity every moment can become a contemporary of God.

This is why we said above that the good is an ontological fact. Love, for example, is more than co-operation, more than feeling and acting together. Love *is* being together, a mode of existence, not only a state of the soul.

The psychological aspect of love, its passion and emotion, is but an aspect of an ontological situation. When man loves man he enters a union which is more than an addition, more than one plus one. To love is to attach oneself to the spirit of unity, to rise to a new level, to enter a new dimension, a spiritual dimension. For, as we have seen, whatever man does to man, he also does to God.

Significantly, the Bible describes love in the following way: "Thou shalt love the Lord, thy God with all thy heart, with all thy soul, with all thy *meod*." What does *meod* mean? It can only mean what it means everywhere in the Bible: the adverb "*very*," "*much*," in a superlative degree. In trying to qualify the verb "to love" the text was suddenly short of expression. Progressively it states: "with all thy heart." And even more: with all thy soul. But even that was not sufficiently expressed until it said: with all thy *veriness* . . .

20 The Essence of Man

All that exists obeys. Man alone occupies a unique status. As a
natural being he obeys, as a human being he must frequently
choose; confined in his existence, he is unrestrained in his will.
His acts do not emanate from him like rays of energy from
matter. Placed in the parting of the ways, he must time and
again decide which direction to take. The course of his life is,
accordingly, unpredictable; no one can write his autobio-
graphy in advance.

Is man, who occupies such a strange position in the great
realm of being, an outcast of the universal order? an outlaw?
a freak of nature? a shred of yarn dropped from nature's loom,
which has since been strangely twisted by the way? Astronomy and geology have taught us to disdain the overweening
vanity of man. Even without the benefit of astronomy and
geology, the psalmist must have been oppressed with a sense
of self-insignificance, when he asked the somber question:

When I consider Thy heavens, the work of Thy fingers; the moon
and the stars, which Thou hast ordained; What is man that Thou art
mindful of him? and the son of man, that Thou visitest him?

(Psalms 8:3–4)

However, if man's value and position in the universe are to be defined as one divided by the infinite, the infinite designating the number of beings which populate the universe; if man $= \frac{1}{\infty}$, how should we account for the fact that infinitesimal man is obviously the only being on this planet capable of making such an equation?

An ant is never stricken with amazement, nor does a star consider itself a nonentity. Immense is the scope of astronomy and geology, yet what is astronomy without the astronomer? What is geology without the geologist?

If we had to characterize an individual like William Shakespeare in terms of a measuring rod, we would surely avail ourselves of Eddington's description of man's position within the universe and say that Shakespeare is almost precisely halfway in size between an atom and a star. To assess his vegetative existence, it is important to know, for example, that man consists of a hundred million cells. However, to assess the essence of man, which alone accounts for the fact of his being anxious to assess his existence, we must discern what is unique about him.

Reflecting about the infinite universe we could perhaps afford to resign ourselves to the trivial position of being a nonentity. However, pondering over our reflection, we discover that we are not only carried and surrounded by the universe of meaning. Man is a fountain of immense meaning, not only a drop in the ocean of being.

The human species is too powerful, too dangerous to be a mere toy or a freak of the Creator. He undoubtedly represents something unique in the great body of the universe: a growth, as it were, an abnormal mass of tissue, which not only began to interact with other parts but also, to some degree, was able to

Man is not alone

modify their very status. What is its nature and function? Is it malignant, a tumor, or is it supposed to serve as a brain of the universe?

The human species shows at times symptoms of being malignant and, if its growth remains unchecked, it may destroy the entire body for the sake of its expansion. In terms of astronomical time, our civilization is in its infancy. The expansion of human power has hardly begun, and what man is going to do with his power may either save or destroy our planet.

The earth may be of small significance within the infinite universe. But if it is of some significance, man holds the key to it. For one thing man certainly seems to own: a boundless, unpredictable capacity for the development of an inner universe. There is more potentiality in his soul than in any other being known to us. Look at an infant and try to imagine the multitude of events it is going to engender. One child called Bach was charged with power enough to hold generations of men in his spell. But is there any potentiality to acclaim or any surprise to expect in a calf or a colt? Indeed, the essence of man is not in what he is, but in what he is able to be.

IN THE DARKNESS OF POTENTIALITY

Yet the darkness of potentiality is the hotbed of anxiety. There is always more than one path to go, and we are forced to be free—we are free against our will—and have the audacity to choose, rarely knowing how or why. Our failures glare like flashlights all the way, and what is right lies underground. We are in the minority in the great realm of being, and, with a genius for adjustment, we frequently seek to join the multitude. We are in the minority within our own nature, and in the agony and battle of passions we often choose to envy the beast. We behave as if the animal kingdom were our lost paradise, to which we are trying to return for moments of delight, believing that it is the animal state in which happiness consists. We have an endless craving to be like the beast, a nostalgic admiration for the animal within us. According to a contemporary scientist: "Man's greatest tragedy occurred when he ceased to walk on all fours and cut himself off from the animal world by assuming an erect position. If man had continued to walk horizontally, and rabbits had learned to walk vertically, many of the world's ills would not exist."

BETWEEN GOD AND THE BEASTS

Man is continuous both with the rest of organic nature and with the infinite outpouring of the spirit of God. A minority in the realm of being, he stands somewhere between God and the beasts. Unable to live alone, he must commune with either of the two.

Both Adam and the beasts were blessed by the Lord, but man was also charged with conquering the earth and dominating the beast. Man is always faced with the choice of listening either to God or to the snake. It is always easier to envy the beast, to worship a totem and be dominated by it, than to hearken to the Voice.

Our existence seesaws between animality and divinity, between that which is more and that which is less than humanity:

below is evanescence, futility, and above is the open door of the divine exchequer where we lay up the sterling coin of piety and spirit, the immortal remains of our dying lives. We are constantly in the mills of death, but we are also the contemporaries of God.

Man is "a little lower than the angels" (Psalm 8:5) and a little higher than the beasts. Like a pendulum he swings to and fro under the combined action of gravity and momentum, of the gravitation of selfishness and the momentum of the divine, of a vision beheld by God in the darkness of flesh and blood. We fail to understand the meaning of our existence when we disregard our commitments to that vision. Yet only eyes vigilant and fortified against the glaring and superficial can still perceive God's vision in the soul's horror-stricken night of human folly, falsehood, hatred and malice.

Because of his immense power, man is potentially the most wicked of beings. He often has a passion for cruel deeds that only fear of God can soothe, suffocating flushes of envy that only holiness can ventilate.

If man is not more than human, then he is less than human. Man is but a short, critical stage between the animal and the spiritual. His state is one of constant wavering, of soaring or descending. Undeviating humanity is nonexistent. The emancipated man is yet to emerge.

Man is more than what he is to himself. In his reason he may be limited, in his will he may be wicked, yet he stands in a relation to God which he may betray but not sever and which constitutes the essential meaning of his life. He is the knot in which heaven and earth are interlaced.

When carried away by the joy of acting as we please, adopting any desire, accepting any opportunity for action if the body welcomes it, we feel perfectly satisfied to walk on all fours. Yet there are moments in every one's life when he begins to wonder whether the pleasures of the body or the interests of the self should serve as the perspective from which all decisions should be made.

BEYOND OUR NEEDS

In spite of the delights that are within our reach, we refuse to barter our souls for selfish rewards and to live without a conscience on the proceeds. Even those who have forfeited the ability for compassion have not forfeited the ability to be horrified at their inability to feel compassion. The ceiling has collapsed, yet the souls still hang by a hair of horror. Time and again everyone of us tries to sit in judgment over his life. Even those who have gambled away the vision of virtue are not deprived of the horror of crime. Through disgust and dismay we struggle to know that to live on selfish needs is to kill what is still alive in our dismay. There is only one way to fumigate the obnoxious air of our world—to live beyond our own needs and interests. We are carnal, covetous, selfish, vain, and to live for the sake of unselfish needs means to live beyond our own means. How could we be more than what we are? How could we find resources that would give our souls a surplus that is not our own? To live beyond our needs means to be independent of selfish needs. Yet how would man succeed in breaking out of the circle of his self?

The possibility of eliminating self-regard ultimately depends on the nature of the self; it is a metaphysical rather than a psychological issue. If the self exists for its own sake, such independence would be neither possible nor desirable. It is only in assuming that the self is not the hub but a spoke, neither its own beginning nor its own end, that such possibility could be affirmed.

Man *is* meaning, but not his own meaning. He does not even know his own meaning, for a meaning does not know what it means. The self *is* a need, but not its own need.

All our experiences are needs, dissolving when the needs are fulfilled. But the truth is, our existence, too, is a need. We are such stuff as needs are made of, and our little life is rounded by a will. *Lasting* in our life is neither passion nor delight, neither joy nor pain, but the answer to a need. The lasting in us is not our will to live. There is a need for our lives, and in living we satisfy it. Lasting is not our desire, but our answer to that need, an agreement not an impulse. Our needs are temporal, while our being needed is lasting.

WHO IS IN NEED OF MAN?

We have started our inquiry with the question of the individual man—what is the meaning of the individual man?—and established his uniqueness in his being pregnant with immense potentialities, of which he becomes aware in his experience of needs. We have also pointed out that he finds no happiness in utilizing his potentialities for the satisfaction of his own needs, that his destiny is to be a need.

But who is in need of man? Nature? Do the mountains stand in need of our poems? Would the stars fade away if astronomers ceased to exist? The earth can get along without the aid of the human species. Nature is replete with opportunity to satisfy all our needs except one—the need of being needed. Within its unbroken silence man is like the middle of a sentence and all his theories are like dots indicating his isolation within his own self.

Unlike all other needs, the need of being needed is a striving to give rather than to obtain satisfaction. It is a desire to satisfy a transcendent desire, a craving to satisfy a craving.

All needs are one-sided. When hungry we are in need of food, yet food is *not* in need of being consumed. Things of beauty attract our minds; we feel the need of perceiving them, yet they are not in need of being perceived by us. It is in such one-sidedness, that most of living is imprisoned. Examine an average mind, and you will find that it is dominated by an effort to cut reality to the measure of the ego, as if the world existed for the sake of pleasing one's ego. Everyone of us entertains more relations with things than with people, and even in dealings with people we behave toward them as if they were things, tools, means to be used for our own selfish ends. How rarely do we face a person as a person. We are all dominated by the desire to appropriate and to own. Only a free person knows that the true meaning of existence is experienced in giving, in endowing, in meeting a person face to face, in fulfilling other people's needs.

When realizing the surplus of what we see over what we feel, the mind is evasive, even the heart is incomplete. Why are we discontent with mere living for the sake of living? Who has made us thirsty for what is more than existence?

Everywhere we are surrounded by the ineffable, our familiarity with reality is a myth. To the innermost in our soul even beauty is an alloy mixed with the true metal of eternity. There is neither earth nor sky, neither spring nor autumn; there is only a question, God's eternal question of man: Where art Thou? Religion begins with the certainty that something is asked of us, that there are ends which are in need of us. Unlike all other values, moral and religious ends evoke in us a sense of obligation. They present themselves as tasks rather than as objects of perception. Thus, religious living consists in serving ends which are in need of us.

Man is not an innocent bystander in the cosmic drama. There is in us more kinship with the divine than we are able to believe. The souls of men are candles of the Lord, lit on the cosmic way, rather than fireworks produced by the combustion of nature's explosive compositions, and every soul is indispensable to Him. Man is needed, he is *a need of God.*

21 The Problem of Ends

In attributing to needs a large share in the genesis of artistic and religious experiences and moral judgments, we are prone to overestimate their importance and to assume that all ideals we know or cherish are projections of our own needs, that acts of justice, creations of beauty are crystallizations of interests—just as ashtrays, shoestrings and fluorescent lamps—and that their value consists in their being desirable.

Looking more closely at our problem, it becomes obvious to us that there is a structural difference between biological * and cultural needs. In the first case the need—or the demand—creates the supply; in the second the supply creates the need. The "interest" society takes in creative art may afford the artists the physical possibilities to produce, but that "interest" itself does not produce art. Did Van Gogh accomplish what he did in answer to the call of would-be purchasers or to the enthusiasm of admirers? Has our own eagerness to see a new Shakespeare, who would express the tension of our age, given birth to genius? Yet, we continue to cling to the theory that art is the product of a need, the artist's need for self-expression or society's need for the enjoyment of art.

* To be distinguished from artificial needs, see above p. 182.

217

Analyze the process of our enjoyment of art. You might mistake it at first as being motivated by the need to find expression for feelings latent in our soul. Yet this would imply that a work of art could not produce an emotion in us if we had not already experienced it in real life; that we would not be capable of responding to a motive if we had not already registered it, though vaguely, in our own heart.

The fact is that we do not turn to art in order to gratify, but in order to foster interests and feelings. A work of art introduces us to emotions which we have never cherished before. It is boring unless we are surprised by it. Great works produce rather than satisfy needs by giving the world fresh craving. By expressing things we were not even aware of, works of art inspire new ends, unanticipated visions.

Or does the creative act of the artist originate in a need for self-expression? It is obvious that an artist who is engaged in satisfying his personal need is of little concern to society. His work becomes relevant to the world when in the process of expression he succeeds in attaining ends which are relevant to others. If Honoré de Balzac were solely interested in satisfying his desire for money and prestige, his achievements would have been pertinent to no one else but him. His significance became universal when he succeeded in creating types and situations, the relevance of which had little to do with his own private needs.

It is not the blind need for self-expression that is the secret of a creative personality. Only he who has nothing to say

218

boasts of his urge for self-expression. There must be something to be expressed, an emotion, a vision, an end, which produces the need for expressing it. The end is the basic number, the need is but the coefficient.

ENDS AND NEEDS

Human life consists of needs as a house consists of bricks, yet an accumulation of needs is no more a life than a heap of bricks is a house. Life as a whole is related to a purpose, to an end. True, unlike a house, man is more than a means to an end, yet it is his relation to ends, his ability to realize that life without ends is not worth living, that seems to indicate the peculiar status of his existence. It is the distinction of man to be concerned with ends not only with needs.

Needs are corelative: they are strivings to achieve or maintain ends, functions of purpose rather than mere outpourings of causes. To define needs without reference to the ends or values upon which they are intent is like assuming that there are normal perceptions with no objects perceived. Needs are man's relation to values and ends. To take an interest is to become aware of such a relation.

Ends are requirements which are often independent of needs. Just as our sense perception does not create but only registers the perceived things, so is a feeling of need merely an inner response to an objective end. Feelings, perceptions are ours; ends, things are the world's; and the world is the Lord's.

Morality and religion do not begin as feelings within man

but as responses to goals and situations outside of man. It is always in regard to an objective situation that we judge and assert it is right or wrong; and it is in answer to what is beyond the ineffable that man says yes to God.

A free man does not look upon himself as if he were a repository of fixed needs, but regards his life as an orientation toward ends. To have a goal before one's eyes, to pursue it and to keep on extending it, seems to be the way of civilized living. It is typical of the debauchee to adjust his ends to his selfish needs. He is always ready to conform to his needs. Indeed, anybody can be taught to have needs and to indulge in costly food, dress or anything which satisfies the appetites or tastes. Yet, free men are not blind in obeying needs but, weighing and comparing their relative merits, they will seek to satisfy those which contribute to the enhancement and enrichment of higher values. In other words, they would approve only of those needs that serve the attainment of good ends. They do not say: "Needs justify the ends," but on the contrary: "Ends justify the needs." To be able to forego the gratification of one need for the sake of another, or for the sake of moral, esthetic or religious principles, they must be, to some degree, independent of needs.

Psychological fatalism which maintains that there is only one way, an animal way, is a paralyzing fallacy to which the spirit of man will never surrender. The mind is not a repository of fixed ideas but rather an orientation toward or a perspective from which the world is apprehended. Nor is the soul a thrall of interests, living under the mesmeric spell of predetermined needs.

There is more than one end on the itinerary of every person's life, some are stations on the road, while others diverge, confusing our ways. Blind to the main goal, we usually stray after selfish or parochial ends, imitating patterns that happen to please us, weaving the web of needs by thoughtlessly interlacing habits and desires.

Much in civilization serves to give stability to, or even to enhance, competitive goals rather than to help the search after spiritual ends. We whitewash murder with our will to live and do not recoil from doing injustice in our zeal to satisfy selfish ambitions.

THE ERROR OF PAN-PSYCHOLOGY

Just as in the Middle Ages sciences were regarded as *ancillae theologiae*, it is claimed today that the problems of metaphysics, religion, ethics and the arts are essentially problems of psychology. There is a tendency which we should like to call *pan-psychology*. It proclaims psychology as capable of explaining the origin and development of the laws, principles and values of logic, religion, and ethics by reducing both form and content of thought and conduct to subjective psychical processes, to impulses and functions of psychical development.

The error of this view lies in its confounding values, laws or principles with the psychical setting in which they come to our attention. It is fallacious to identify the content of knowledge with the emotional reactions which accompany its acquisition, or concepts with mental functions. Our affirming or denying a conclusion, our saying yes or no to an idea, is an act in which we claim to assert the truth on the basis of either logical cogency or intuitive certainty. It is precisely the immunity to emotion that enables us to entertain a claim to knowing the truth.

Such a claim is entertained by the pan-psychologist himself. Laws must be applied by him to the vague, manifold and chaotic psychological processes if they are to be classified, interpreted and made intelligible. But such laws, to be universally valid, must be capable of being logically and epistemologically defended; they must be categories, not psychical processes themselves. Otherwise they would be merely additional subject matter for psychological analysis without any cognitive value. Are we not, then, compelled to admit that there are cognitive acts the validity of which is independent of impulses?

From the point of view of pan-psychology we would have to deny it. Yet we have no more right to say that logical categories are the offspring of impulses than to say that impulses are the offspring of categories. Categories are facts of human consciousness which are just as undeniably given as impulses. We seem, in fact, to be more dependent on categories in trying to understand impulses than we are in need of impulses in developing our categories.

THE CONSCIOUSNESS OF GOOD AND EVIL

Good and evil are not psychological concepts, although the ways in which they are understood are affected by the psychological conditions of the human personality, just as the particular forms in which they are realized are often determined by historical, political and social conditions. However, good and

222

evil as such do not denote functions of the soul or society but goals and ends and are, in their essence, independent of the psychical chain of causation.*

In his consciousness of good and evil or in complying with religious precepts even at the price of frustrating personal interests, man does not regard his attitude as a mere expression of a feeling: he is sure of reflecting objective *requiredness*, of striving for a goal which is valid regardless of his own liking. Should we, against the empirical fact of such consciousness, condemn it as wishful thinking or rather say that our theories about the relativity of all moral goals result from a time-conditioned decline of attentiveness to ultimate goals?

Man's consciousness of requiredness is, of course, no proof that the particular forms in which he tries to attain his moral or religious ends are absolutely valid. However, the fact of such consciousness may serve as an index of his being committed to striving for valid ends. Man's conception of these ends is subject to change; his being committed endures forever.

Moral actions may, of course, be explained on selfish grounds. As a social being the welfare of an individual depends upon the welfare of all other members of the group. Any service, therefore, that extends beyond the confines of my direct needs would be an investment in my own personal welfare. Altruism would be egoism in disguise, and moral deeds not different from the generous service any intelligent merchant extends to his customers. Sacrificing my own interests for the sake of another man would be merely another example of the kind of self-denial I exercise in regard to my own interests, denying to myself the satisfaction of some needs

* See above p. 120.

in order to attain the satisfaction of others. To adjust my conduct to the interests of other people as far as it would ultimately suit me would be all I am morally bound to do.

Yet what constitutes the consciousness of good and evil, of right and wrong is the requiredness to act not for my own sake, to do the right even if no advantage would accrue to myself. The expediency of a good deed may serve as an incentive to carry out a moral obligation, yet it is certainly not identical with it.

GOD'S SECRET WEAPON

Man's life is not only driven by a centripetal force revolving around the ego, but is also impelled by centrifugal forces outward from the ego-center. His acts are not only self-regarding but also self-surpassing.

Even in the pursuit of private ends, man is often compelled to establish or to advance universal values. It is as if man stood under a command to employ his abilities for unselfish stakes, a command which he is obliged to listen to and suffers for disregarding. That command is not the product but the origin of civilization. Civilized living is the result of that urge, of that drive to proceed in our efforts beyond immediate needs, beyond individual, tribal or national goals.

The urge to build a family, to serve society or dedicate oneself to art and science, may often originate in the desire to satisfy one's own appetite or ambition. Yet, seen from the watchtower of history, the selfish usefulness of required deeds,

224

the possibility of regarding them as instrumental to the attainment of one's own selfish goals, is God's secret weapon in his struggle with man's callousness.

We often have the false joy of believing that others are serving us, while, in truth, it is we who serve others. Our individual mind is not the measure of meaning. For whom does he plant who plants a tree? For generations to come, for faces he has never seen. Higher purposes are shrewdly disguised as ends of immediate usefulness. It is as if a *divine cunning* operated in human history, using our instincts as pretexts for the attainment of goals which are universally valid, a scheme to harness man's lower forces in the service of higher ends.

Goodness does not consist in being an object of interest, in being enjoyed or desired by some or most people. An action is not good because we are pleased with it or because we think it is good. As noted above, good and evil are relations within reality. Good is that which God cares for; good is that which *unites* man within himself, which unites man and man, man and God.

LIFE IS TRIDIMENSIONAL

Life is tridimensional, every act can be evaluated by two co-ordinate axes, the abscissa is man, the ordinate is God. Whatever man does to man, he also does to God. To those who are attentive to Him who is beyond the ineffable, God's relation to the world is an actuality, an absolute implication of being, the ultimate in reality, obtaining even if at this moment it is not perceived or acknowledged by anybody; those who reject or betray it do not diminish its validity.

The right or the morally good is an end that surpasses our experience of needs. It is beyond the power of an emotion to sense adequately the supreme grandeur of the moral end; our efforts to express it are conditioned by the limitations of our nature. And still the vision of that absolute grandeur is not always lost. In studying the history of man's attempts to implement the moral end, we must not confound his vision with his interpretation. Man's understanding of *what* is right and wrong has often varied throughout the ages; yet the consciousness *that* there is a distinction between right and wrong is permanent and universal. In formulating laws, he often fumbles and fails to find adequate ways of implementing justice or to preserve all the time a clear grasp of its meaning. Yet even when forfeiting his vision, he does not quite lose an awareness of what was once in his sight. He knows that justice is a standard to which his laws must conform in order to deserve the name of justice. We know of no tribe, of no code that would insist that it is good to hate or that it is right to injure each other. Justice is something which all men are able to esteem.

In order to retain that vision alive, we must try to preserve and augment the sense of the ineffable, to remember constantly the superiority of our task to our will and to keep aflame our awareness of living in the great fellowship of all beings, in which we are all equal before the ultimate. Conformity to the ego is no longer our exclusive concern, for we become concerned with another problem—how to fulfill what is asked of us.

The universe is not a waif and life is not a derelict. Man is

226

neither the lord of the universe nor even the master of his own destiny. Our life is not our own property but a possession of God. And it is this divine ownership that makes life a sacred thing.

What we have said about justice applies to religion as well. His own heart is not the source of that light in which the pious man sees his simple words becoming signals of eternity. Hands do not build the citadel in which the pious man takes shelter when all towers are tottering. The reality of the holy is not dependent upon his will to believe. Religion would not rule the heart if it were simply an achievement of his mind or an outgrowth of his sentiments.

22 What Is Religion?

There is a perpetual temptation for the analytic mind to classify religion under strict heads, to seal its facts with preconceived labels, as if reality had to fit the handy trade-marks of our theories, as if that which cannot be compared and stamped as mana, tabu, totem, or the like, must be ignored or denied. Every particular act of faith or ritual is, furthermore, analyzed as if it were a bank account, a matter of calculation, wherein every detail is explainable and every transaction a computable operation.

Having attained supreme critical detachment from their subject matter, some scholars apply to religion a paleontological method, as if it were a fossil chiseled from the shale or a plant brought home by an expedition from exotic lands. Indeed, when taken out of the depth of piety, it exists mostly in a symbiosis with other values like beauty, justice or truth.

Some students of religion operate with categories gained by anthropological observers of primitive beliefs and rituals, as if the total character, the genuine nature of humanity were revealed in its primitive stage. They seem to be guided by a doctrine that glorifies the primeval man who was natural and

229

unspoiled by the arts of civilized life. As a result, they insist upon understanding the prophets in terms of the savage.

It was a basic tenet of older anthropology that in primitive society there was no place for the spontaneous activity of the individual, that the thoughts and actions of the individual were always imposed on him by social pressures. That tenet is the underlying assumption of the sociological theory in which society, its demands and instincts for survival are looked upon as the mystic cause of religion.

That tenet has been discarded by present-day anthropology, which claims that even on the low levels of civilization the individual was not completely oppressed. To us it seems obvious that the great ideas were born in spite of social pressure, in spite of circumstance. Moses had to wage a battle not only against Pharaoh but also against his own people. Upon the masses which clamored for a golden calf the prohibition to make a graven image had to be imposed. The essence of religion lies beyond the grasp of sociology.

Psychology of religion, on the other hand, idealizing neutral and indifferent informants, claims to attain an understanding of religion by submitting questionnaires to a typical group of people or by taking the views and mentality of an average person as a perspective of judgment. But can lack of bias ever compensate for absence of insight? Is indifference the same as objectivity?

How do we gain an adequate concept of history or astronomy? We do not turn to the man in the street, but to those who devote their life to research, to those who are trained in scientific thought and have absorbed all the data about the subject. For an adequate concept of religion, we likewise should turn to those whose mind is bent upon the spiritual, whose life *is* religion and who are able to discern between truth and happiness, between spirit and emotion, between faith and self-reliance.

From the point of view of a mind to which the enigmatic holiness of religion is not a certainty but a problem, we can hardly expect more than an extruitive understanding, a glimpse from afar of what is to the pious man compellingly present and overwhelmingly real.

Experts on religion are in danger of resembling the proverbial yeshivah-student who claimed to understand and master all arts. Asked whether he could swim, he replied: "I do not know how to swim, but I understand swimming . . ."

We encounter a similar situation with people who apply themselves to prosody and are experts in scanning meters. They boast of a craft that comes easily to the naturally gifted poet. Unlike the experts, the poet, though he knows how to compose perfect poetry may not be able to teach the theory of verse-making. He is, however, capable of teaching someone, who like him is naturally gifted, with a slight hint. Thus sparks are kindled in the souls of people open to religion by the words of the pious, sparks which become luminous in their hearts.*

IS RELIGION A FUNCTION OF THE SOUL?

Those who cannot free themselves from the idea that morality and religion are man's own response to a selfish need, the result of a craving for security and immortality, or the attempt to conquer fear, are not unlike people who presume that rivers,

* Judah Halevi, Kusari V.16.

like canals, were constructed by man for the purpose of navigation. It is true that economic needs and political factors have taught man to exploit the waterways. But are the rivers themselves the products of human genius?

Most people assume that we feed our body in order to ease the pangs of hunger, to calm the irritated nerves of an empty stomach. As a matter of fact, we eat not because we feel hungry but because the intake of food is essential for the maintenance of life, supplying the energy necessary for the various functions of the body. Hunger is the signal for eating, its occasion and regulator, not its true cause. Let us not confound the river with navigation, nutrition with hunger, or religion with the use which man makes of it.

Psychological theories claiming that religion originated in a feeling or a need seem to overlook that such a cause does not have the efficacy to produce religion. They fail to see that since, for example, the feeling of absolute dependence or the fear of death entirely lacks any religious quality, its relation to religion cannot be that of cause and effect. Such a feeling may contribute to man's receptivity of religion, but is itself incapable of creating it. Since the authentic religious intention associated with such a feeling must be derived from another source, it is obvious that those theories fail to enucleate the issue.

MAGIC AND RELIGION

The essence of religion does not lie in the satisfaction of a human need. It is true that man, seeking to exploit the forces

232

of nature for his own profit, does not recoil from forcing supernatural beings to do his pleasure. But such intentions and practices are characteristic, not of religion, but of magic, which is "the next of kin to science" and the deadly enemy of religion, its very opposite.

While it is impossible to prove that magic has everywhere preceded religion and that, by recognizing its inherent false-hood, the "age of magic" gave place to the "age of religion," the survival of magic within religion is a fact too apparent to be overlooked. Its danger to religion was recognized in the Pentateuch, where it is most emphatically condemned as a heinous sin, as well as by the prophets in whose eyes it was tantamount to idolatry and by the rabbis who took stern measures to eliminate it from Jewish life. And the fight had to be continued through the ages.

Abraham was not going to sacrifice his only son in order to satisfy a personal need, nor did Moses accept the Decalogue for the sake of attaining happiness. The second command-ment: "Thou shalt not make unto thee a graven image," has, in fact, defied rather than satisfied the "religious needs" of many people throughout the ages. Nor were the prophets eager to please, or to be in agreement with, popular sentiments. Prophetic religion may be characterized as the very opposite of opportunism.

To define religion primarily as a quest for personal satisfac-tion or salvation is to make it a refined kind of magic. As long as man sees in religion the satisfaction of his own needs, a guarantee for immortality or a device to protect society, it is not God whom he serves but himself. The more removed from the ego, the more real is His presence. It is a sure way of missing Him when we think that God is an answer to a human need, as if not only armies, factories and movies, but God, too, had to cater to the ego.

There have always been people who thought that "it is expedient that there should be gods, and since it is expedient, let us believe that gods exist" (Ovid, *Ars Amatoria*, Book 1. l.637). It was to such people that Amos addressed himself.

> Woe unto you that long for the day of the Lord!
> Wherefore would you have the day of the Lord?
> It is darkness, and not light.
> As if a man fled from a lion,
> And a bear met him;
> He ran into the house
> and leaned his hand on the wall,
> and a serpent bit him.
> Is not the day of the Lord darkness rather than light?
> pitch-dark and not a ray of light?
>
> (Amos 5:18-20)

To believe in God is to fight for Him, to fight whatever is against Him within ourselves, including our interests when they collide with His will. Only when, forgetting the ego, we begin to love Him, God becomes our need, interest and concern. But the way to love leads through fear lest we transgress His unconditional command, lest we forget His need for man's righteousness.

THE OBJECTIVE SIDE OF RELIGION

Every investigation springs out of a basic question, which sets the rudder of our mind. Yet the number of questions available for our research is limited. They are conventionally

234

repeated in almost every scientific investigation. Like tools, they are handed down from one scholar to another. Not through our own eyes do we look at the world, but through lenses ground by our intellectual ancestry. But our eyes are strained and tired of staring through spectacles worn by another generation. We are tired of overlooking entities, of squinting at their relations to other things. We want to face reality as it is and not to ask only: What is its cause? What is its relation to its sources? to society? to psychological motives? We are tired of dating and comparing. Indeed, when the questions that were once keen and penetrating are worn out, the investigated object no longer reacts to the inquiry. Much depends upon the driving force of a new question. The question is an invocation of the enigma, a challenge to the examined object, provoking the answer. A new question is more than the projection or vision of a new goal; it is the first step toward it. To know what we want to know is the first prerequisite of research.

Modern man seldom faces things as they are. In the interpretation of religion, our eyes are bent toward its bearing upon various realms of life rather than upon its own essence and reality. We investigate the relation of religion to economics, history, art, libido. We ask for its origin and development, for its effect upon psychical, social and political life. We look upon religion as if it were an instrument only, not an entity. We forget to inquire: What is religion itself? The objective aspect of religion is usually left in the background. In the foreground looms large and salient its subjective supplement, the human response. We heed the resonance and ignore the bell, we peer into religiosity and forget religion, we behold the experience and disregard the reality that antecedes

235

the experience. To understand religion through the analysis of the sentiments it instills is to miss its essence. It is as if we were to apprehend a work of art by describing our impression of it rather than by grasping its intrinsic value. The inner value of a work of art subsists regardless of our responsiveness to it. The essence of a work of art is neither tantamount to nor commensurable with the impression it produces, with what is reflected in the enjoyment of art. The stratum of inner experience and the realm of objective reality do not lie on the same level.

THERE IS NO NEUTRALITY

To restrict the world of faith to the realm of human endeavor or consciousness would imply that a person who refuses to take notice of God could isolate himself from Him. But there is no neutrality before God; to ignore means to defy him. Even the emptiness of indifference breeds a concern, and the bitterness of blasphemy is a perversion of a regard for God. The world of faith is neither the outgrowth of imagination nor the product of will. It is not an inner process, a feeling or a thought, and should not be looked upon as a bundle of episodes in the life of man. To assume that man stands before God for the duration of an experience, meditation or performance of a ritual, is absurd. Man's relation to God is not an episode. What is going on between God and man is for the duration of life.

Religion as an institution, the Temple as an ultimate end, or, in other words, religion for religion's sake, is idolatry. The fact is that evil is integral to religion, not only to secularism. Parochial saintliness may be an evasion of duty, an accommodation to selfishness.

Religion is for God's sake. The human side of religion, its creeds, rituals and institutions, is a way rather than the goal. The goal is "to do justice, to love mercy and to walk humbly *with* thy God." When the human side of religion becomes the goal, injustice becomes a way.

THE HOLY DIMENSION

What gives rise to faith is not a sentiment, a state of mind, an aspiration, but an everlasting fact in the universe, something which is prior to and independent of human knowledge and experience—*the holy dimension* of all existence. The objective side of religion is the spiritual constitution of the universe, the divine values invested in every being and exposed to the mind and will of man; an ontological relation. This is why the objective or the divine side of religion eludes psychological and sociological analysis.

All actions are not only agencies in the endless series of cause and effect; they also affect and concern God, with or without human intention, with or without human consent. All existence stands in the dimension of the holy and nothing can be conceived of as living outside of it. All existence stands before God—here and everywhere, now and at all times. Not only a vow or conversion, not only the focusing of the mind upon God, engages man to Him; all deeds, thoughts, feelings and events are His concern.

237

Just as man lives in the realm of nature and is subject to its laws, so does he find himself in the holy dimension. He can escape its bounds as little as he can take leave of nature. He can sever himself from the dimension of the holy neither by sin nor by stupidity, neither by apostasy nor by ignorance. There is no escape from God.

PIETY IS A RESPONSE

To have faith is consciously to enter a dimension in which we abide by our very existence. Piety is a response, the subjective corelative of an objective condition, the awareness of living within the holy dimension, the realization that what starts as an experience *in* man transcends the human sphere, becoming an objective event outside of himself. In this power of transcending the soul, time and space, the pious man sees the distinction of religious acts. If, to our minds, prayer were only the articulation of words, of nothing but psychological relevance and of no metaphysical resonance, nobody would waste his time in an hour of crisis by praying in self-delusion.

It is man's very existence that stands in relation to God. Man's relations to state, society, family, etc., do not penetrate all strata of his personality. In his final solitude, in the hour of approaching death, they are blown away like chaff. It is in the dimension of the holy, that he abides, whatever befalls him.

Man is not alone

We are prone to be impressed by the ostentatious, the obvious. The strident caterwaul of the animal fills the air, while the still small voice of the spirit is heard only in the rare hours of prayer and devotion. From the streetcar window we may see the hunt for wealth and pleasure, the onslaught upon the weak, faces expressing suspicion or contempt. On the other hand, the holy lives only in the depths. What is noble retires when exposed to light, humility is extinguished in the awareness of it, and the willingness for martyrdom rests in the secrecy of the things to be. Walking upon the clay, we live in nature, surrendering to impulse and passion, to vanity and arrogance, while our eyes reach out to the lasting light of truth. We are subject to terrestrial gravitation, yet we are confronted by God.

In the dimension of the holy the spiritual is a bridge flung across a frightful abyss, while in the realm of nature the spiritual hovers like the wafted clouds, too tenuous to bear man across the abyss. When a vessel sails into a typhoon and the maw of the boiling maelstrom opens to engulf the tottering prey, it is not the pious man, engrossed in supplication, but the helmsman who intervenes in the proper sphere with proper means, fighting with physical tools against physical powers. What sense is there in imploring the mercy of God? Words do not stem the flood, nor does meditation banish the storm. Prayer never entwines directly with the chain of physical cause and effect; the spiritual does not interfere with the natural order of things. The fact that man with undaunted

239

sincerity pours into prayer the best of his soul springs from the conviction that there is a realm in which the acts of faith are puissant and potent, that there is an order in which things of spirit can be of momentous consequence.

There are phenomena which appear irrelevant and accidental in the realm of nature but are of great meaning in the dimension of the holy. To worship violence, to use brutal force, is natural, while sacrifice, humility and martyrdom are unheard of from the point of view of nature. It is in the domain of the holy that a thought or a sentiment may stand out as an everlasting approach to truth, where prayers are steps toward Him *aere perennior*.

We live not only in time and space but also in the knowledge of God, being near Him not only through our faith but, first of all, through our life. All events reflect in Him; all existence is coexistence with God. Time and space are not the limits of the world. Our life occurs here and in the knowledge of God.

23 A Definition of Jewish Religion

We have tried to understand religion as a universal phenomenon. It is now our task to define the Jewish conception of religion. As noted above, religion—its human side—begins with a sense of obligation, "with the awareness that something is asked of us," with the consciousness of an ultimate commitment. It is furthermore an awareness of "God who sues for our devotion, constantly, persistently, who goes out to meet us as soon as we long to know Him." Accordingly, religious consciousness is to be characterized by two features—it must be a consciousness of an *ultimate commitment* and it must be a consciousness of *ultimate reciprocity*.

There is only one way to define Jewish religion. It is the *awareness of God's interest in man*, the awareness of a *covenant*, of a responsibility that lies on Him as well as on us. Our task is to concur with His interest, to carry out His vision of our task. God is in need of man for the attainment of His ends, and religion, as Jewish tradition understands it, is a way of serving these ends, of which we are in need, even though we may not be aware of them, ends which we must learn to feel the need of.

241

Life is a *partnership* of God and man; God is not detached from or indifferent to our joys and griefs. Authentic vital needs of man's body and soul are a divine concern. This is why human life is holy. God is a partner and a partisan in man's struggle for justice, peace and holiness, and it is because of His being in need of man that He entered a *covenant* with him for all time, a mutual bond embracing God and man, a relationship to which God, not only man, is committed.

This day you have avowed the Lord to be your God, promising to walk in His ways, to obey His rules and commandments, and to hearken to His voice; And this day the Lord has avowed you to be His very own people, as He has promised you, and to obey His commandments.

(Deuteronomy 26:17-18)

Some people think that religion comes about as a perception of an answer to a prayer, while in truth it comes about in our knowing that God shares our prayer. The essence of Judaism is the awareness of the *reciprocity* of God and man, of man's *togetherness* with Him who abides in eternal otherness. For the task of living is His and ours, and so is the responsibility. We have rights, not only obligations; our ultimate commitment is our ultimate privilege.

In interpreting Malachi 3:18, Rabbi Aha ben Ada said: "Then shall ye again discern between the righteous and the wicked," meaning: "between him who has faith and him who has no faith"; "between him that serveth God and him that serveth Him not," meaning: "between him who serves God's *need* and him who does not serve God's *need*. One should not make of the Torah a spade with which to dig, a tool for personal use or a crown to magnify oneself" (Midrash Tehillim, ed. Buber, p. 240f).

242

His need is a self-imposed concern. God is now in need of man, because He freely made him a partner in His enterprise, "a partner in the work of creation." "From the first day of creation the Holy One, blessed be He, longed to enter into *partnership* with the terrestrial world" to dwell *with* His creatures within the terrestrial world. (Numbers Rabba, ch. 13,6; compare Genesis Rabba ch. 3,9.) Expounding the verse in Genesis 17:1, the Midrash remarked: "In the view of Rabbi Johanan we need His honor; in the view of Rabbi Simeon ben Lakish He needs our honor" (Genesis Rabba, ch. 30; unlike Theodor, p. 277).

"When Israel performs the will of the Omnipresent, they add strength to the heavenly power; as it is said: 'To God we render strength' (Psalms 60:14). When, however, Israel does not perform the will of the Omnipresent, they weaken—if it is possible to say so—the great power of Him who is above; as it is written, 'Thou didst weaken the Rock that begot Thee.'" (Pesikta, ed. Buber, XXVI, 166b; compare the two versions.)

Man's relationship to God is not one of passive reliance upon His Omnipotence but one of active assistance. "The impious rely on their gods . . . the righteous are the support of God." (Genesis Rabba, ch. 69,3.)

The Patriarchs are therefore called "the chariot of the Lord." (Genesis Rabba, ch. 47,6; 82,6.)

> He glories in me, He delights in me;
> My crown of beauty He shall be.
> His glory rests on me, and mine on Him;
> He is near to me, when I call on Him.
> (*The Hymn of Glory*)

The extreme boldness of this paradox was expressed in a Tannaitic interpretation of Isaiah 43:12: "Ye are my witnesses, saith the Lord, and I am God"—when you are my witnesses I am God, and when you are not my witnesses I am not God.*

THE DIVINE PATHOS

The God of the philosophers is all indifference, too sublime to possess a heart or to cast a glance at our world. His wisdom consists in being conscious of Himself and oblivious to the world. In contrast, the God of the prophets is all concern, too merciful to remain aloof to His creation. He not only rules the world in the majesty of His might; He is personally concerned and even stirred by the conduct and fate of man. "His mercy is upon all His works" (Psalms 145:9).

These are the two poles of prophetic thinking: The idea that God is one, holy, different and apart from all that exists, and the idea of the inexhaustible concern of God for man, at times brightened by His mercy, at times darkened by His anger. He is both transcendent, beyond human understanding, and full of love, compassion, grief or anger.

God does not judge the deeds of man impassively, in a spirit of cool detachment. His judgment is imbued with a feeling of intimate concern. He is the father of all men, not only a judge; He is a lover engaged to His people, not only a king. God stands in a passionate relationship to man. His love or anger, His mercy or disappointment is an expression of His profound participation in the history of Israel and all men.

Prophecy, then, consists in the proclamation of the divine *pathos*, expressed in the language of the prophets as love,

* Sifre Deuteronomy, 346; compare the interpretation of Psalms 123:1.

mercy or anger. Behind the various manifestations of His pathos is one motive, one need: The divine need for human righteousness.

The pagan gods had animal passions, carnal desires, they were more fitful, licentious than men; the God of Israel has a passion for righteousness. The pagan gods had selfish needs, while the God of Israel is only in need of man's integrity. The need of Moloch was the death of man, the need of the Lord is the life of man. The divine pathos which the prophets tried to express in many ways was not a name for His essence but rather for the modes of His reaction to Israel's conduct which would change if Israel modified its ways.

The surge of divine pathos, which came to the souls of the prophets like a fierce passion, startling, shaking, burning, led them forth to the perilous defiance of people's self-assurance and contentment. Beneath all songs and sermons they held conference with God's concern for the people, with the well, out of which the tides of anger raged. *

The Bible is not a history of the Jewish people, but the story of God's quest of the righteous man. Because of the failure of the human species as a whole to follow in the path of righteousness, it is an individual—Noah, Abraham—a people: Israel—or a remnant of the people, on which the task is bestowed to satisfy that quest by making every man a righteous man.

There is an eternal cry in the world: God is beseeching man. Some are startled; others remain deaf. We are all looked for. An air of expectancy hovers over life. Something is asked of man, of all men.

* See A. Heschel, *Die Prophetie*, Cracow, 1936, pp. 56-87; 127-180.

For thousands of years the deity and darkness were thought to be the same: a being, self-attached and full of blind desires; a being whom man revered but did not trust; that would reveal itself to the mad but not to the meek. For thousands of years it was accepted as a fact that the ultimate deity was hostile to man and could only be appeased by offerings of blood, until the prophets came who could not bear any more to see the defeat of God at the hands of fear, and proclaimed that darkness was His abode, not His essence; that as bright as midday's sun was His voice giving an answer to the question: What does God desire?

Is it music?

> Take away from me the noise of your songs,
> And to the melody of your lyres I will not listen.
> (Amos 5:23)

Is it prayer?

> When you spread out your hands,
> I will hide my eyes from you;
> Though you make many a prayer,
> I will not listen.
> Your hands are full of bloodshed—
> (Isaiah 1:15-16)

Is it sacrifice?

Does the Lord delight in burnt-offerings and sacrifices as much as in obedience to the voice of the Lord?

> (I Samuel 15:22)

Man is not alone

And now, O Israel, what does the Lord your God require of you but to stand in awe of the Lord your God, walk in His ways, love Him, serve the Lord your God with all your mind and heart, and keep the commands of the Lord and His statutes that I am commanding you today, for your good?

(Deuteronomy 10:12)

THE RELIGIOUS NEED

Religion, it is almost generally acknowledged, corresponds to a particular need of the human personality. Just as there are needs for health and wealth, for knowledge and beauty, for prestige and power, there is a need for religion. Such an interpretation of religion, to be valid, must prove the religious need to be different from all other needs and to be incapable of being satisfied in any other but its own way. It must further demonstrate that just as nonreligious goals, like power, wealth and prestige, cannot be attained through religion, the religious need cannot be satisfied through the pursuit of these nonreligious goals.

To satisfy nonreligious needs we seek to exploit the forces of nature to our advantage. But do we seek to exploit anything in order to satisfy our religious needs? What, then, is the way of satisfying the religious need? What are the ends man is striving to attain in religion?

There is, indeed, in every human being an unquenchable need for the lasting, an urge to worship and to revere. Divergence begins in the object and manner of worship. Yet that unquenchable need is often miscarried into self-aggrandizement or a desire to find a guarantee for personal immortality. Juda-

247

ism shows it to be a need *to be needed by God*. It teaches us that every man is in need of God because God is in need of man. Our need of Him is but an echo of His need of us.

There is, of course, the constant danger of believing what we wish rather than wishing what we believe, of cherishing our need as God rather than adopting God as our need. This is why we must always appraise our needs in the light of divine ends.

THE UNKNOWN ENDS

It is natural and common to care for personal and national goals. But is it as natural and common to care for other people's needs or to be concerned with universal ends? Conventional needs like pleasure are easily assimilated by social osmosis. Spiritual needs have to be implanted, cherished and cultivated by the vision of their ends. We do not have to rise above ourselves in order to dream of being strong, brave, rich, of being rulers of an empire or "a kingdom of soldiers." But we have to be inspired in order to dream God's dream: "Thou shalt be holy, for I thy God am holy." . . . "Thou shalt be unto Me a kingdom of priests, a holy people."

It is God who teaches us our ultimate ends. Abraham may not have felt the need for abandoning home and country, nor were the people of Israel eager to give up the flesh-pots of Egypt for the prospect of going into the wilderness.

Analyzing man's potentialities, it becomes evident that his uniqueness and essential meaning lie in his ability to satisfy ends that go beyond his ego, while his natural concern is: What

248

may others do for my ego? Religion teaches him to ponder about what he may do for others and to realize that no man's ego is worthy of being the ultimate end.

There is an ancient hymn with which we conclude our daily prayers and which gives expression to our conception of ultimate ends. It is a hymn which may be regarded as the national anthem of the Jewish people.

We hope therefore, Lord our God, soon to behold thy majestic glory, when the abominations shall be removed from the earth, and the false gods exterminated; when the world shall be perfected under the reign of the Almighty, and all mankind will call upon thy name, and all the wicked of the earth will be turned to thee. May all the inhabitants of the world realize and know that to thee every knee must bend, every tongue must vow allegiance. May they bend the knee and prostrate themselves before thee, Lord our God, and give honor to thy glorious name; may they all accept the yoke of thy kingdom, and do thou reign over them speedily forever and ever. For the kingdom is thine, and to all eternity thou wilt reign in glory, as it is written in thy Torah: "The Lord shall be King forever and ever." And it is said: "The Lord shall be King over all the earth; on that day the Lord shall be One, and his name One."

THE CONVERSION OF ENDS INTO NEEDS

Jewish religious education consists in converting ends into personal needs rather than in converting needs into ends, so that, for example, the end to have regard for other people's lives becomes my concern. Yet, if those ends are not assimilated as needs but remain mere duties, uncongenial to the heart, incumbent but not enjoyed, then there is a state of tension between the self and the task. The perfectly moral act bears a seed within its flower: the sense of objective requiredness within the subjective concern. Thus, justice is good not because we feel the need of it; rather we ought to feel the need of justice because it is good.

Religions may be classified as those of self-satisfaction, of self-annihilation or of fellowship. In the first worship is a quest for satisfaction of personal needs like salvation or desire for immortality. In the second all personal needs are discarded, and man seeks to dedicate his life to God at the price of annihilating all desire, believing that human sacrifice or at least complete self-denial is the only true form of worship. The third form of religion, while shunning the idea of considering God a means for attaining personal ends, insists that there is a partnership of God and man, that human needs are God's concern and that divine ends ought to become human needs. It rejects the idea that the good should be done in self-detachment, that the satisfaction felt in doing the good would taint the purity of the act. Judaism demands the full participation of the person in the service of the Lord; the heart rather than boycotting the acts of the will ought to respond in joy and undivided delight.

THE PLEASURE OF GOOD DEEDS

Pleasure, though not the spring, may and ought to be the by-product of moral or religious action. The good or the holy is not necessarily that which I do not desire, and the feeling of pleasure or gratification does not divest a good deed of its quality of goodness. The heart and the mind are rivals but not

250

irreconcilable enemies, and their reconciliation is a major end in striving for integrity. It is true that the idea of justice and the will to justice are not twin-born. But a moral person is a partisan who loves the love of good. It is not true that love and obedience cannot live together, that the good never springs from the heart. To be free of selfish interests does not mean to be neutral, indifferent, or to be devoid of interests, but, on the contrary, to be a partisan of the self-surpassing. God does not dwell beyond the sky. He dwells, we believe, in every heart that is willing to let Him in.

The sense of moral obligation remains impotent unless it is stronger than all other obligations, stronger than the stubborn power of selfish interests. To compete with selfish inclinations the moral obligation must be allied with the highest passion of the spirit.

To be stronger than evil, the moral imperative must be more powerful than the passion for evil. An abstract norm, an ethereal idea, is no match for the gravitation of the ego. Passion can only be subdued by stronger passion.

From the fact that an end is adopted and cherished as a personal interest, it does not follow that the end was of psychological origin, just as our utilization of the quantum theory does not prove that it came about as the result of utilitarian motives. Thus, the fact of God becoming a human need does not vitiate the objectivity and validity of the idea of God.

The solution to the problem of needs lies not in fostering a need to end all needs but in fostering a need to calm all other needs. There is a breath of God in every man, a force lying deeper than the stratum of will, and which may be stirred to become an aspiration strong enough to give direction and even to run counter to all winds.

24 The Great Yearning

All thoughts and feelings about the tangible and knowable world do not exhaust the endless stirring within us. There is a surplus of restlessness over our palpable craving. We are lonely with men, with things, with our own cravings. The goals are greater than the grasp.

Man is in travail with God's dreams and designs.

What is the essence of our feeling for God? May it not be defined as a yearning that knows no satisfaction, as a yearning to meet that which we do not even know how to long for?

We are used to living with ephemeral desires, but we also know that life is a little higher than our daily interests, that when we sigh self-complacency away a joy comes over us that is not only ours. Bereaved of delusive satisfactions, our hearts become drunk with an endless yearning which our minds cannot fully apprehend.

Like the vital power in ourselves that gives us the ability to fight and to endure, to dare and to conquer, which drives us to experience the bitter and the perilous, there is an urge in wistful souls to starve rather than be fed on sham and distortion. To the pious man God is as real as life, and as nobody

253

would be satisfied with mere knowing or reading about life, so he is not content to suppose or to prove logically that there is a God; he wants to feel and to give himself to Him; not only to obey but to approach Him. His desire is to taste the whole wheat of spirit before it is ground by the millstone of reason. He would rather be overwhelmed by the symbols of the inconceivable than wield the definitions of the superficial.

Stirred by a yearning after the unattainable, a pious man is not content with being confined to what he is. His desire is not only to *know* more than what ordinary reason has to offer, but to *be* more than what he is; to transform the soul into a vessel for the transcendent, to grasp with the senses what is hidden from the mind, to express in symbols what the tongue cannot speak and what the reason cannot conceive, to experience as a reality what vaguely dawns in intuitions.

THE NOBLE NOSTALGIA

The yearning for spiritual living, the awareness of the ubiquitous mystery, the noble nostalgia for God, have rarely subsided in the Jewish soul. It has found many and varied expressions in ideas and doctrines, in customs and songs, in visions and aspirations. It is part of the heritage of the psalmists and prophets. Listen to the psalmist: "As the hart panteth after the water brooks, so panteth my soul after Thee, O Lord. My soul thirsteth for God, for the living God; when shall I come and appear before God?" (42:2-3). "My soul yearneth, yea even pineth for the courts of the Lord; my heart and my flesh sing for joy unto the Living God" (84:3). "For a day in Thy courts is better than a thousand" (84:11). "In Thy presence is fulness of joy" (16:11).

Is Judaism an earthly religion? "I am a sojourner in the earth" (119:19), the psalmist declares. "Whom have I in heaven but Thee? And beside Thee I desire none upon earth" (73:25). "My flesh and my heart faileth; but God is the rock of my heart and my portion forever" (73:26). "But as for me, the nearness of God is my good" (73:28). "O God, Thou art my God; earnestly will I seek Thee; my soul thirsteth for Thee, my flesh longeth for Thee in a dry and weary land, where no water is . . . for Thy lovingkindness is better than life. My soul is satisfied as with marrow and fatness; . . . I remember Thee upon my couch and meditate on Thee in the nightwatches . . . My soul cleaveth unto Thee, Thy right hand holdeth me fast" (63:2, 4, 6, 7, 9).

Awareness of God is incompatible with self-righteousness, with the conceits of taking one's achievements too seriously. "If I be wicked, woe unto me; And if I be righteous, yet will I not lift up my head. I am full of ignomy; see Thou mine affliction" (Job 10:15).

There are many laws in the Bible demanding the offering of sacrifices at the sanctuary. Yet although the prophets insist that the true "sacrifices of God are a broken spirit, a broken and contrite heart" (Psalms 51:19), there is no commandment to be contrite. For is it necessary to issue such a precept? How is it possible not to be sick at heart in a world such as this?

> The earth is given into the hands of the wicked . . .
> The tabernacles of robbers prosper,
> And they that provoke God are secure.
>
> (Job 9:24; 12:6)

Self-contentment is something which is too hard to bear together with the knowledge of coexisting woe. Who could feel that one's own ugly failures would be wiped off with petty excuse or be happy in pleading moral incapacity?

> Is not thy wickedness great?
> And thine iniquities infinite? . . .
> Thou hast not given water to the weary to drink,
> And Thou hast withholden bread from the hungry.
> And as a mighty man, who hath the earth,
> And as a man of rank, who dwelleth in it,
> Thou hast sent widows away empty,
> And the arms of the fatherless have been broken.
>   (Job 22:5, 7-9)

"Nothing is as whole as a broken heart." The sense of contrition should not impair the awareness of our spiritual might, of the eternal nobility that goes with eternal responsibility.

A learned man lost all his sources of income and was looking for a way to earn a living. The members of his community, who admired him for his learning and piety, suggested to him to serve as their cantor on the Days of Awe. But he considered himself unworthy of serving as the messenger of the community, as the one who should bring the prayers of his fellow-men to the Almighty. He went to his master the Rabbi of Husiatin and told him of his sad plight, of the invitation to serve as a cantor on the Days of Awe, and of his being afraid to accept it and to pray for his congregation.

"*Be* afraid, and pray," was the answer of the rabbi.

Man is not alone

The aim of Jewish piety lies not in futile efforts toward the satisfaction of needs in which one chances to indulge and which cannot otherwise be fulfilled, but in the maintenance and fanning of a discontent with our aspirations and achievements, in the maintenance and fanning of a craving that knows no satisfaction. Thus, Judaism is the cause rather than the result of a need; an objective requirement rather than a subjective interest. It teaches man never to be pleased, to despise satisfaction, to crave for the utmost, to appreciate objectives to which he is usually indifferent. It plants in him a seed of endless yearning, a need of spiritual needs rather than a need of achievements, teaching him to be content with what he *has*, but never with what he *is*.

Most of us are unhappy, not because we are dissatisfied with what we are—for example, callous to other people's distress or privation—but because of our being discontent with what we possess. Religion is the source of dissatisfaction with the self.

Happiness, as was noted above, is not a synonym for either satisfaction, complacency or smugness, but is essentially the certainty of being needed, of having the vision of the goal which is still to be attained. It is self-satisfaction which breeds futility and despair.

Animals are satiable and pleased with themselves, while men are only capable of being satisfied with themselves when their spirit begins to decay and to stick in the morass of overrated deeds. Self-satisfaction, self-fulfillment, is a myth which panting souls must find degrading. All that is creative stems from a seed of endless discontent. It is because of men's dissatisfaction with the customs, sanctions and modes of behavior of their age and race that moral progress is possible. New insight begins when satisfaction comes to an end, when all that has been seen or said looks like a distortion to him who sees the world for the first time.

Self-contentment is the brink of the abyss, from which the prophets try to keep us away. Even while the people of Israel were still in the desert, before entering the Promised Land, they were warned to brave the perils of contentment. "When I bring them into the land which I swore to their fathers to give them, a land abounding in milk and honey, and they eat their fill and wax fat, and turn to alien gods, and serve them, despising Me, breaking My covenant . . ." (Deuteronomy 31:20). For this is the way of languid downfall:

> Jeshurun grew fat, and kicked—
> Thou didst grow fat, thick, gorged.
> (Deuteronomy 32:15)

If we should try to portray the soul of a prophet by the emotions that had no place in it, contentment would be mentioned first. The prophets of Israel were like geysers of disgust, disturbing our conscience till this day, urging us to be heartsick for the hurt of others.

> Woe to them that are at ease in Zion,
> And trust in the mountain of Samaria . . .
> That lie upon beds of ivory,
> And stretch themselves upon their couches,
> And eat the lambs out of the flock,
> And the calves out of the midst of the stall;
> That chant to the sound of the viol,
> And invent to themselves instruments of music, like David;

258

Man is not alone

That drink wine in bowls,
And anoint themselves with the finest oils;
But they are not heart-sick for the hurt of Joseph.

(Amos 6; 1, 4-6)

ASPIRATIONS

Together with the potentialities locked up in our nature we possess the key to release and develop them. The key is our aspirations. To attain any value, we must anticipate, seek and crave for it. A stone does not strive to become a statue, and when transformed into a statue, the form is forced upon it rather than anticipated. Yet man lives not by needs alone but by aspirations for that which he does not even know how to utter.

A person *is* what he aspires for. In order to know myself, I ask: What are the ends I am striving to attain? What are the values I care for most? What are the great yearnings I should like to be moved by?

He who is satisfied has never truly craved, and he who craves for the light of God neglects his ease for ardor, his life for love, knowing that contentment is the shadow not the light. The great yearning that sweeps eternity is a yearning to praise, a yearning to serve. And when the waves of that yearning swell in our souls all the barriers are pushed aside: the crust of callousness, the hysteria of vanity, the orgies of arrogance. For it is not the I that trembles alone, it is not a stir out of my soul but an eternal flutter that sweeps us all.

No code, no law, even the law of God, can set a pattern for all of our living. It is not enough to have the right ideas. For the will, not reason, has the executive power in the realm of living. The will is stronger than reason and does not blindly submit to the dictates of rational principles. Reason may force the mind to accept intellectually its conclusions. Yet what is the power that will make me love to do what I ought to do?

A young man became an apprentice to a blacksmith. He learned how to hold the tongs, how to lift the sledge, how to smite the anvil and how to blow the fire with the bellows. Having finished his apprenticeship, he was chosen to be employed at the smithery of the royal palace. However, the young man's delight came soon to an end, when he discovered that he had failed to learn how to kindle a spark. All his skill and knowledge in handling the tools were of no avail.

25 A Pattern for Living

It is a bitter observation: Life is constant peril; moral or even physical security is a myth. Few of us know what to do with our lives, with our power and will, with our intelligence and freedom. The heart is frail and blind; unguided, it becomes savage and forlorn.

It is easier to cope with viruses and germs than with callousness of heart or with imperceptible inner decay. Unaided, what would we do except trample and impair? Who would attend us when we were about to wreck that which no man can ever reconstruct?

Our hearts do not breed the desire to be righteous or holy. While the mind is endowed with a capacity to grasp higher ends and to direct our attention to them, regardless of any material advantage, the will is naturally inclined to submit to selfish ends, regardless of the mind's insights. There is nothing which is less reliable than man's power for self-denial.

Nor is the mind ever immune to the subtle persuasions of the vested interests of the self. The ultimate goals remain, therefore, either unapprehended or unvoiced by the mind. It is religion that must articulate the unvoiced.

Peace with all our needs would mean surrender to the ego. It is easy to convert the soul into a madhouse and think it is a sanctuary. The spirit that gasps for a breath of the divine, to be stronger than the ruthlessness of passions, must be equipped with weapons that the mind alone cannot produce.

Man's cry for inner freedom goes together with a feeling of disgust with artificial needs. Every one of us, at one time or another, realizes the wisdom of the ancient maxim "that to have no wants is divine; to have as few as possible comes next to the divine" (Diogenes Laertius, Socrates, sec. 11). While only saints can be like Rabbi Hanina, about whom every day a heavenly voice issues from Mount Horeb and proclaims: "All the world is nourished for the sake of My son, Hanina, but my son, Hanina, is satisfied with a small measure of carobs from the Sabbath-eve to the next Sabbath-eve" (Berakot 17b), it is possible for all men to accept the advice that "we should aim rather at leveling down our desires than leveling up our means."

NEITHER DEIFYING NOR VILIFYING

Throughout the ages two extreme views about our problem have most frequently been voiced—one deifying desire, the other vilifying it. There were those who, overwhelmed by the dark power of passion, believed that they sensed in its raving a manifestation of the gods and celebrated its gratification as a sacred ritual. Dionysian orgies, fertility rites, sacred prostitution are extreme examples of a view that subconsciously has never died out.

The exponents of the other extreme, frightened by the destructive power of unbridled passion, have taught man to see ugliness in desire, Satan in the rapture of the flesh. Their advice was to repress the appetites, and their ideal, self-renunciation and asceticism. Some Greeks said: "Passion is a god, Eros"; Buddhists say: "Desire is evil."

To the Jewish mind, being neither enticed nor horrified by the powers of passion, desires are neither benign nor pernicious but, like fire, they do not agree with straw. They should be neither quenched nor supplied with fuel. Rather than worship fire and be consumed by it, we should let a light come out of the flames. *Needs are spiritual opportunities.*

SPIRIT AND FLESH

Allegiance to Judaism does not imply defiance of legitimate needs, a tyranny of the spirit. Prosperity is a worthy goal of aspiration and a promised reward for good living. Although there is no celebration of our animal nature, recognition of its right and role is never missing. There is an earnest care for its welfare, needs and limitations.

Judaism does not despise the carnal. It does not urge us to desert the flesh but to control and to counsel it; to please the natural needs of the flesh so that the spirit should not be molested by unnatural frustrations. We are not commanded to be pyromaniacs of the soul. On the contrary, a need that serves the enhancement of life, without causing injury to anyone else, is the work of the Creator, and the wanton or ignorant destruction or defacement of His creation is vandalism. "It is indeed God's gift to man, that he should eat and drink and be happy as he toils" (Ecclesiastes 3:13).

Good living obviously implies control and the relative conquest of passions, but not the renunciation of all satisfaction. Decisive is not the act of conquest but how the victory is utilized. Our ideal is not ruthless conquest but careful alteration of needs. Passion is a many-headed monster, and the goal is achieved through painstaking metamorphosis rather than by amputation or mutilation.

Judaism is not committed to a doctrine of original sin and knows nothing of the inherent depravity of human nature. The word "flesh" did not assume in its vocabulary the odor of sinfulness; carnal needs were not thought of as being rooted in evil. Nowhere in the Bible is found any indication of the idea that the soul is imprisoned in a corrupt body, that to seek satisfaction in this world means to lose one's soul or to forfeit the covenant with God, that the allegiance to God demands renunciation of worldly goods.

Our flesh is not evil but material for applying the spirit. The carnal is something to be surpassed rather than annihilated. Heaven and earth are equally His creation. Nothing in creation may be discarded or abused. The enemy is not in the flesh; it is in the heart, in the ego.

To the Bible good is equated with life. Being is intrinsically good. "God saw it was good." The Torah is conceived as a "Tree of Life," advancing the equation of life and goodness; "In the way of righteousness is life" (Proverbs 12:28).

Man is not alone

There is no conflict between God and man, no hostility between spirit and body, no wedge between the holy and the secular. Man does not exist apart from God. The human is the borderline of the divine.

Life passes on in proximity to the sacred, and it is this proximity that endows existence with ultimate significance. In our relation to the immediate we touch upon the most distant. Even the satisfaction of physical needs can be a sacred act. Perhaps the essential message of Judaism is that in doing the finite we may perceive the infinite. It is incumbent on us to obtain the perception of the impossible in the possible, the perception of life eternal in everyday deeds.

God is not hiding in a temple. The Torah came to tell inattentive man: "You are not alone, you live constantly in holy neighborhood; remember: 'Love thy neighbor—God—as thyself.'" We are not asked to abandon life and to say farewell to this world, but to keep the spark within aflame, and to suffer His light to reflect in our face. Let our greed not rise like a barrier to this neighborhood. God is waiting on every road that leads from intention to action, from desire to satisfaction.

Man is endowed with the ability of being superior to his own self. He does not have to feel helpless in the face of the "evil inclination." He is capable of conquering evil; "God made man upright." If you ask: "Why did He create the 'evil inclination'?" . . . Says the Lord: "You turn it evil." *

* Tanhuma, Bereshit No. 7.

265

One can serve God with the body, with his passions even with "the evil impulse" (Sifre Deuteronomy, § 32); one must only be able to distinguish between the dross and the gold. This world acquires flavor only when a little of the other world is mingled with it. Without nobility of spirit, the flesh may, indeed, become a focus of darkness.

The road to the sacred leads through the secular. The spiritual rests upon the carnal, like "the spirit that hovers over the face of the water." Jewish living means living according to a system of checks and balances.

THE HOLY WITHIN THE BODY

Holiness does not signify an air that prevails in the solemn atmosphere of a sanctuary, a quality reserved for supreme acts, an adverb of the spiritual, the distinction of hermits and priests. In his great Code, Maimonides, unlike the editor of the Mishnah, named the section dealing with the laws of the Temple-cult The Book of Service, while the section dealing with the laws of chastity and diet he named The Book of Holiness. The strength of holiness lies underground, in the somatic. It is primarily in the way in which we gratify physical needs that the seed of holiness is planted. Originally the holy (*kadosh*) meant that which is set apart, isolated, segregated. In Jewish piety it assumed a new meaning, denoting a quality that is involved, immersed in common and earthly endeavors; carried primarily by individual, private, simple deeds rather than public ceremonies. "Man should always regard himself as if the Holy dwelled within his body, for it is written: 'The

266

Holy One is within you' (Hosea 11:9), therefore one should not mortify his body" (Taanit 11b).

Man is the source and the initiator of holiness in this world. "If a man will sanctify himself a little, God will sanctify him more and more; if he sanctified himself below, he will be sanctified from above" (Yoma 39a).

Judaism teaches us how even the gratification of animal needs can be an act of sanctification. The enjoyment of food may be a way of purification. Something of my soul may be drowned in a glass of water, when its content is gulped down as if nothing in the world mattered except my thirst. But we can come a bit closer to God, when remembering Him still more in excitement and passion.

Sanctification is not an unearthly concept. There is no dualism of the earthly and the sublime. All things are sublime. They were all created by God and their continuous being, their blind adherence to the laws of necessity are, as noted above, a way of obedience to the Creator. The existence of things throughout the universe is a supreme ritual.

A man alive, a flower blooming in the spring, is a fulfillment of God's command: "Let there be!" In living we are directly doing the will of God, in a way which is beyond choice or decision. This is why our very existence is contact with His will; why life is holy and a responsibility of God as well as man.

NOT TO SACRIFICE BUT TO SANCTIFY

The giver of life did not ask us to despise our brief and poor life but to ennoble it, not to sacrifice but to sanctify it. Rabbi

267

Hananyah ben Akashyah said: "The Holy One, blessed be He, desired to purify Israel; hence He gave them Torah and many mitzvoth [ways of conduct], as it is said: The Lord was pleased, for the sake of [Israel's] righteousness, to render the Torah great and glorious (Isaiah 42:21).* Before fulfilling a commandment, we bless and praise Him 'who hast sanctified us with Thy commandments.' On Shabbat and holidays we pray: 'Sanctify us with Thy commandments.'"

To the votaries of the ancient orgiastic cults wine was an intoxicant used to stimulate frenzy, "that which makes man delirious" (Herodotus 4.79). To ascetics wine is pernicious, a source of evil. To the Jews wine is more than anything else associated with the term and act of sanctification (Kiddush). Over wine and bread we invoke the sanctity of the Shabbat. "Sanctify thyself in things that are permitted to you" (Yebamot 20a), not only in ritual, in ways prescribed by the Torah." "In all thy ways know Him" (Proverbs 3:6).

Sanctification as a reason for walking in His ways is not a concept of religious pragmatism—the theory according to which the tangible effects would serve as the criteria for the validity of commandments. The good is to be done for God's sake, not for the furtherance of man's perfection.

"It says: 'The wise man's eyes are in his head' (Ecclesiastes 2:4). Where, it may be asked, should they be if not in his head? . . . What it means, however, is this. We have learned that a man should not go four cubits with his head uncovered, the reason being that the Shechinah rests on the head. Now a wise man's eyes . . . are directed to his head, to that which rests on his head, and then he knows that the light which is kindled on his head requires oil, for the human body is a wick

* Mishnah Makkot 3, 16.

and the light is aflame above it. And the king Solomon calls and says: 'and let thy head lack no oil' (Ecclesiastes 9:8), for the light above his head requires oil, which consists in good deeds, and therefore the eyes of a wise man are towards his head, and no other place." (Zohar III, 187a.)

NEEDS AS MITZVOT

We are taught that man is needed, that our authentic needs are divine requirements, symbols of cosmic needs. God is the subject of all subjects. Life is His and ours. He has not thrown us out into the world and abandoned us. He shares in our toil; He is partner to our anxieties. A man in need is not the exclusive and ultimate subject of need: God is in need with him. Becoming conscious of a need, one has to ask himself: Is God in need with me? To have God as a partner to one's actions is to remember that our problems are not exclusively our own. Jewish existence is living shared with God.

LIVING WITHIN AN ORDER

The quest for right living, the question of what is to be done right now, right here, is the authentic core of Jewish religion. It has been the main theme of Jewish literature, from the prophets till the times of the Hasidim, and it has been explored with a sense of urgency, as if life were a continuous state of emergency.

269

With quiet sadness and rich with strenuous lessons of defeat, we learn today to understand that there are no extemporaneous solutions to perpetual problems; that the only safeguard against constant danger is constant vigilance, constant guidance. Such guidance, such vigilance is given to him who lives in the shadows of Sinai; whose weeks, days, hours are set in the rhythm of the Torah.

What constitutes the Jewish form of living is not so much the performance of single good deeds, the taking of a step now and then, as the pursuit of a way, being on the way; not so much the acts of fulfilling as the state of being committed to the task, of belonging to an order in which single deeds, aggregates of religious feeling, sporadic sentiments, moral episodes become parts of a complete pattern.

ALL OF LIFE

The pious man believes that all events are secretly interrelated; that the sweep of all we are doing reaches beyond the horizon of our comprehension; that everything in history throws its weight into the scales of God's balance; that every deed denotes a degree in the gauge of the holy, irrespective of whether the man who performs it is aiming at this goal or not. It is just the nonritual, the secular conditions, which the prophets of Israel regarded as being a divine concern. To them the totality of human activities, social and individual, of all inner and external circumstances, is the divine sphere of interest. The domain of the Torah is therefore all of life, the trite as well as the sacred.

Man is not alone

THE UNHEROIC

Judaism is a theology of the common deed, of the trivialities of life, dealing not so much with the training for the exceptional as with the management of the trivial. The predominant feature in the Jewish pattern of life is unassuming, inconspicuous piety rather than extravagance, mortification, asceticism. Thus, the purpose seems to be to ennoble the common, to endow worldly things with hieratic beauty; to attune the comparative to the absolute, to associate the detail with the whole, to adapt our own being with its plurality, conflicts and contradictions, to the all-transcending unity, to the holy.

THE INNER AUTHORITY

Psychic life, too, is a constant process of growth and waste, and its needs cannot be satisfied by scanty, desultory injections. Not being a hibernating animal, man cannot live by what he stores away. He may have a full memory and an empty soul. Unfree men are horrified by the suggestion of accepting a spiritual regimen. Associating inner control with external tyranny, they would rather suffer than be subject to spiritual authority. Only free men, those who are not prone to canonize every caprice, do not equate self-restraint with self-surrender, knowing that no man is free who is not a master of himself, that the more liberties we enjoy, the more discipline we need.*

* See A. J. Heschel, *The Earth Is the Lord's*, New York 1950, p. 63.

271

Laissez-faire, the absence of control or government in the private realm, is a dream. Inner life is populated by numerous insatiable and competitive forces. There can be no power vacuum. Where principles are suppressed, a petty desire climbs to power. The immense realm of living, if it is not to be stultified, cannot be placed under the control of either ethics or jurisprudence. How to invest man with the ability to master all of life is a supreme challenge to intelligence.

The answer to that challenge is a life of piety, and it is the pious man to whom we must turn in order to learn how to live.

26 The Pious Man

From time immemorial, piety has been esteemed as one of the more precious ideals of human character. At all times, and in all places, men have striven to acquire piety, and no effort or sacrifice has seemed too great if they could attain it. Was this a mere illusion on their part, a flight of the imagination? No! It was a real virtue—something solid, clearly to be seen and of real power. Thus, as a specific fact of existence met with in life, it is something which indisputably deserves examination. That it is commonly neglected or overlooked by scientific research is due partly to the methodological difficulties involved in an approach to such a subject, but more fundamentally to the fact that it has theological aspects, which are somewhat repellent to the modern mind. To some piety suggests escape from normal life, an abandonment of the world, seclusion, a denial of cultural interests, and is associated with an old-fashioned, clerical, unctuous pattern of behavior. To others the word suggests prudishness, if not hypocrisy and fanaticism, or seems symptomatic of an attitude toward life which is unhealthy and, indeed, absurd. They feel that such an attitude as that of piety is to be rejected in the interests of mental health and spiritual freedom.

273

Yet the pious man is still with us. He has not vanished from the earth. Indeed, more frequently than is generally realized, situations in normal life are to be encountered which are full of the evidence of pious devotion. The presence of piety amongst us is thus an incontestable fact; so why should prejudice deter us from investigating this phenomenon and, at least, endeavoring to understand it?

THE METHOD OF ANALYSIS

To begin with, we may ask: What is piety? Is it some psychical disposition or quality of the spirit? Is it a state of mind? or an attitude? or a praxis? What are its essential features? What are its meaning and value? What is its significance? What are its aspirations? Is it a unique phenomenon, or is it an accidental circumstance concomitant with other events of human life? What is the inner life of a pious man like? What are the underlying concepts, and what are the apprehensions that are realized in acts of piety?

In an analysis such as this we should not discuss that implicit faith which is involved in general systems of faith and worship but is not acquired independently by individuals; nor should we attempt to scrutinize critically any doctrine or creed. Our purpose, rather, should be to analyze the pious man, and to examine, not his position with regard to any specific form of institutionalized religion, but his attitudes toward the elemental forces of reality. What does God mean in his life? What is his attitude toward the world, toward life, toward his inner forces as well as toward his possessions?

274

Piety is not a psychological concept. The word belongs as little to psychological nomenclature as do the logical concepts of true and false, the ethical concepts of right and wrong or the esthetic concepts of beautiful and ugly. Piety does not denote a function, but an ideal, of the soul. Like wisdom or truthfulness, it is subject to the individual character of a man, being colored by his qualities. Thus, there is a passionate as well as a sober type of piety, an active as well as a quietistic type, an emotional as well as an intellectual one. Yet, in spite of the fact that piety is never independent of the psychical structure of the individual, it is futile to attempt to explain it by any bent or bias of the mental life. It is far from being the result of any psychical dispositions or organic functions. Certain dispositions may influence or intensify it, but they do not create it.

As an act, piety belongs to the stream of the psychical life. However, its spiritual content is not identical with the act itself. It is universal and should be distinguished from the subjective psychical function. Piety is an objective spiritual way of thinking and living. There have been times in which piety was as common as knowledge of the multiplication table is today.

In order to understand piety, we must analyze the consciousness that accompanies the acts of a pious man and to classify the concepts latent in his mind. There is hardly any need for us to emphasize the fact that the validity of such an analysis is not impaired by the possibility that the concepts derived from a general inquiry may not be found present in every act or example of piety. The fact that a poet proves to be unacquainted with the rules that govern his art, or does not apply them in every poem, does not mean that there are no rules for the writing of poetry.

For our purpose we need not be concerned with the psychological aspects of the question. These have their own importance but would require a special investigation. Our purpose is to direct our attention to those essential, constitutive elements that are common to different types of piety, disregarding accidental colorings and the unimportant accompanying circumstances which may differ in different cases. Our task will be to describe piety as it is, without claiming to explain it or to suggest its derivation from other phenomena. We shall not analyze psychologically the course it runs, or its peculiarities as they appear in the life of an individual. We shall not attempt to trace its development historically through the ages and in the matrix of different civilizations, but shall, rather, try to expound its spiritual content, and set forth its concepts and its manifestations in relation to the main realities of common life.

AN ATTITUDE OF THE WHOLE MAN

To label piety as an ability, a potential quality of the soul, would be like defining architecture as a skill. It is impossible to understand facts by mere speculation as to their origins. We should likewise go astray if we labeled it as a mood, an emotional state, a flutter of romantic feeling. To do this would be like characterizing the light of the moon as melancholy, or judging navigation by its danger to human life. Again, to call it a moral or intellectual virtue would be like trying to nail down the shadow of an escaping horse, and so securing neither horse nor shadow. Piety does not consist in isolated acts, in sporadic, ephemeral experiences; nor is it limited to a single stratum of the soul. Although manifesting itself in particular acts, it is beyond the distinctions between intellect and emotion, will and action. Its source seems to lie deeper than the reach of reason and to range farther than consciousness. While it reveals itself in single attitudes such as devotion, reverence, or the desire to serve, its essential forces lie in a stratum of the soul far deeper than the orbit of any of these. It is something unremitting, persistent, unchanging in the soul, a perpetual inner attitude of the whole man. Like a breeze in the atmosphere, it runs through all the deeds, utterances and thoughts; it is a tenor of life betraying itself in each trait of character, each mode of action.

THE ONLY LIFE WORTH LIVING

Piety points to something beyond itself. As it works in the inner life, it keeps ever referring us to something that transcends man, something that goes beyond the present instant, something that surmounts what is visible and available. Steadily preventing man from immersing himself in sensation or ambition, it stands staunchly as the champion of something more important than interest and desires, than passion or career. While not denying the charm and beauty of the world, the pious man realizes that life takes place under wide horizons, horizons that range beyond the span of an individual life or even the life of a nation, of a generation or even of an era.

277

His sight perceives something indicative of the divine. In the small things he senses the significant, in the common and the simple he senses the ultimate; in the rush of the passing he feels the stillness of the eternal. While piety stands in relation to what man knows and feels about the horizons of life, it exceeds by far the sum total reached by adding up his diverse intellectual and emotional experiences. Its essence, in fact, stands for something more than a theory, a sentiment or a conviction. To those who adhere to it, piety is compliance with destiny, the only life worth living, the only course of life that does not eventually throw man into bestial chaos.

Piety is thus a mode of living. It is the orientation of human inwardness toward the holy. It is a predominant interest in the ultimate value of all acts, feelings and thoughts. With his heart open to and attracted by some spiritual gravitation, the pious man moves, as it were, toward the center of a universal stillness, and his conscience is so placed as to listen to the voice of God.

Every man's life is dominated by certain interests and is essentially determined by the aspiration toward those things which matter to him most. The pious man's main interest is concern for the concern of God, which thus becomes the driving force controlling the course of his actions and decisions, molding his aspirations and behavior. It is fallacious to see in isolated acts of perception or consideration the decisive elements in human behavior. Actually, it is the direction of mind and heart, the general interest of a person, that leads him to see or discover certain situations and to overlook others. Interest is, as we have seen above, a selective apprehension based on prior ideas, preceding insights, recognitions or predilections. The interest of a pious man is determined by his faith, so that piety is faith translated into life, spirit embodied in a personality.

THE INNER ANONYMITY

Piety is the direct opposite of selfishness. Living as he does in the vision of the unutterably pure, the pious man turns his back on his own human vanity, and longs to surrender the forces of egotism to the might of God. He is aware of both the shabbiness of human life and the meagerness and insufficiency of human service; and so, to protect the inner wholesomeness and purity of devotion from being defiled by interference from the petty self, he strives toward self-exclusion, self-forgetfulness and an inner anonymity of service. He desires to be unconscious that it is he who is consecrating himself to the service of God. The pious man lays no claim to reward. He hates show, or being conspicuous in any way, and is shy of displaying his qualities even to his own mind. He is engrossed in the beauty of that which he worships, and dedicates himself to ends the greatness of which exceeds his capacity for adoration.

NOT A HABIT

Piety is not a habit, running along in a familiar groove. It is rather an impulse, a spurt, a stirring of the self. Apart from a certain ardor, zeal, intentness, vigor or exertion, it becomes a stunted thing. No one who has even been once impelled by its force will ever entirely shake off its pursuing drive. In moments of stress the pious man may stumble; he may blunder or go astray; he may temporarily succumb in his weakness to the agreeable instead of holding to the true, follow the ostentatious instead of the simple and hard, but his adherence to the holy will only slacken, it will never break away. Such lapses, indeed, are often followed by a new sweep toward the goal, the lapse providing new momentum.

WISDOM AND PIETY

Although piety implies a certain spiritual profundity, it is not an outgrowth of innate intelligence. Its forces spring from purity of heart rather than from acumen of mind. To be pious does not necessarily mean to be sagacious or judicious. It does, however, as a prevailing trend, show features that are peculiar to wisdom, in the ancient sense of that term. Both piety and wisdom involve self-command, self-conquest, self-denial, strength of will and firmness of purpose. But though these qualities are instrumental in the pursuit of piety, they are not its nature. It is the regard for the transcendent, the devotion to God, that constitute its essence. To the pious man, as to the wise one, mastery over self is a necessity of life. Unlike the wise man, however, the pious man feels that he himself is not the autonomous master, but is rather a mediator who administers his life in the name of God.

Man is not alone

Piety not only accepts the mystery but attempts to match it in human endeavor, venturing to lift the human to the level of the spiritual. This should not be called an experience, but the acting upon experience; not a concern about meaning and its exploration, but an attempt to balance life with an accepted meaning.

The pious man is alive to what is solemn in the simple, to what is sublime in the sensuous; but he is not aiming to penetrate into the sacred. Rather he is striving to be himself penetrated and actuated by the sacred, eager to yield to its force, to identify himself with every trend in the world which is toward the divine. To piety it is not the outlook that carries weight but the impression; not the notion but the sentiment; not acquaintance but appreciation; not knowledge but veracity. Piety is not a thinking about coming but a real approach. It is not identical with the performance of rites and ceremonies, but is rather the care and affection put into their performance, the personal touch therein, the offering of life. Piety is the realization and verification of the transcendent in human life.

Piety is a matter of life, not only a sense for the reality of the transcendent, but the taking of an adequate attitude toward it; not only a vision, a way to belief, but adjustment, the answer to a call, a mode of life. Piety stands entirely within the subjective and originates in human initiative. Piety is usually preceded by faith, and it is then faith's achievement, an effort to put faith's ideas into effect, to follow its suggestions. Piety desires not merely to learn faith's truth, but to agree with it;

not merely to meet God, but to abide by Him, agree with His will, echo His words, and respond to His voice.

It is through piety that there comes a revelation of the higher self, the disclosure of what is most delicate in the human soul, the unfolding of the purest elements in the human venture. Essentially, it is an attitude toward God and the world, toward men and things, toward life and destiny.

IN THE PRESENCE OF GOD

The pious man is possessed by his awareness of the presence and nearness of God. Everywhere and at all times he lives as in His sight, whether he remains always heedful of His proximity or not. He feels embraced by God's mercy as by a vast encircling space. Awareness of God is as close to him as the throbbing of his own heart, often deep and calm but at times overwhelming, intoxicating, setting the soul afire. The momentous reality of God stands there as peace, power and endless tranquility, as an inexhaustible source of help, as boundless compassion, as an open gate awaiting prayer. It sometimes happens that the life of a pious man becomes so involved in God that his heart overflows as though it were a cup in the hand of God. This presence of God is not like the proximity of a mountain or the vicinity of an ocean, the view of which one may relinquish by closing the eyes or removing from the place. Rather is this convergence with God unavoidable, inescapable; like air in space, it is always being breathed in, even though one is not always aware of continuous respiration.

Man is not alone

To dwell upon those things which are stepping stones on the path to the holy, to be preoccupied with the great and wondrous vision of His presence, does not necessarily mean an avoidance of the common ways of life, or involve losing sight of worldly beauty or profane values. Piety's love of the Creator does not exclude love of the creation, but it does involve a specific approach to all values. God is before all things, and all values are looked at through Him. Mere splendor of appearance does not appeal to the man of piety. He is bent upon what is good in the eyes of God, and holds as valuable that which stands in accord with His peace. He is not deceived by the specious nor dissuaded by the unseemly. Shining garments, a smiling countenance, or miracles of art do not enchant him when they cover vice or blasphemy. The most magnificent edifices, most beautiful temples and monuments of worldly glory are repulsive to him when they are built by the sweat and tears of suffering slaves, or erected through injustice and fraud. Hypocrisy and pretense of devoutness are more distasteful to him than open iniquity. But in the roughened, soiled hands of devoted parents, or in the maimed bodies and bruised faces of those who have been persecuted but have kept faith with God, he may detect the last great light on earth.

A LIFE COMPATIBLE WITH THE PRESENCE OF GOD

Whatever the pious man does is linked to the divine; each smallest trifle is tangential to His course. In breathing he uses

283

His force; in thinking he wields His power. He moves always under the unseen canopy of remembrance, and the wonderful weight of the name of God rests steadily on his mind. The word of God is as vital to him as air or food. He is never alone, never companionless, for God is within reach of his heart. Under affliction or some sudden shock, he may feel temporarily as though he were on a desolate path, but a slight turn of his eyes is sufficient for him to discover that his grief is outweighed by the compassion of God. The pious man needs no miraculous communication to make him aware of God's presence; nor is a crisis necessary to awaken him to the meaning and appeal of that presence. His awareness may be overlaid momentarily or concealed by some violent shift in consciousness, but it never fades away. It is this awareness of ever living under the watchful eye of God that leads the pious man to see hints of God in the varied things he encounters in his daily walk; so that many a simple event can be accepted by him both for what it is and also as a gentle hint or kindly reminder of things divine. In this mindfulness he eats and drinks, works and plays, talks and thinks; for piety is a life compatible with God's presence.

THE VALUE OF REALITY

This compatibility reveals itself in the way in which he regards and evaluates all phenomena. Man is by nature inclined to evaluate things and events according to the purpose they serve. In the economic life a man is estimated according to his efficiency, by his worth in labor and by his social standing.

Man is not alone

Here every object in the universe is regarded as a commodity or a tool, its value being determined by the amount of work it can perform or the degree of pleasantness it can confer, so that utilization is the measure of all things. But was the universe created merely for the use of man, for the satisfaction of his animal desires? Surely it is obvious how crude and, indeed, thoughtless it is to subject other beings to the service of our interests, seeing that every existence has its own inner value, and that to utilize them without regard to their individual essence is to desecrate them and despise their real dignity. The folly of this instrumental approach is manifest in the vengeance which inevitably follows. In treating everything else as an instrument, man eventually makes himself the instrument of something he does not understand. By enslaving others, he plunges himself into serfdom, serving war lords or those prejudices which come to be imposed upon him. Often, indeed, he wastes his life in serving passions which others shrewdly excite in him, fondly believing that this is his indulgence of his freedom.

The inner value of any entity—men or women, trees or stars, ideas or things—is, as a matter of fact, not entirely subject to any purposes of ours. They have a value in themselves quite apart from any function which makes them useful to our purposes. This is particularly true of man, for it is his essence, that secret of his being in which both existence and meaning are rooted, that commands our respect; so that even though we knew no way in which he might be useful, or no means of subordinating him to any end or purpose, we should esteem him for that alone.

Further, piety is an attitude toward all of reality. The pious man is alert to the dignity of every human being, and to those bearings upon the spiritual value which even inanimate things inalienably possess. Being able to sense the relations of things to transcendent values, he will be incapable of disparaging any of them by enslaving them to his own service. The secret of every being is the divine care and concern that are invested in it. In every event there is something sacred at stake, and it is for this reason that the approach of the pious man to reality is in reverence. This explains his solemnity and his conscientiousness in dealing with things both great and small.

REVERENCE

Reverence is a specific attitude toward something that is precious and valuable, toward someone who is superior. It is a salute of the soul; an awareness of value without enjoyment of that value, or seeking any personal advantage from it. There is a unique kind of transparence about things and events. The world is seen through, and no veil can conceal God completely. So the pious man is ever alert to see behind the appearance of things a trace of the divine, and thus his attitude toward life is one of expectant reverence.

Because of this attitude of reverence, the pious man is at peace with life, in spite of its conflicts. He patiently acquiesces

in life's vicissitudes, because he glimpses spiritually their potential meaning. Every experience opens the door into a temple of new light, although the vestibule may be dark and
dismal. The pious man accepts life's ordeals and its need of
anguish, because he recognizes these as belonging to the totality of life. Such acceptance does not mean complacency
or fatalistic resignation. He is not insensitive. On the contrary he is keenly sensitive to pain and suffering, to adversity
and evil in his own life and in that of others; but he has the
inner strength to rise above grief, and, with his understanding
of what these sorrows really are, grief seems to him a sort of
arrogance. We never know the ultimate meaning of things,
and so a sharp distinction between what we deem good or bad
in experience is unfair. It is a greater thing to love than to
grieve, and, with love's awareness of the far-reachingness of all
that affects our lives, the pious man will never overestimate the
seeming weight of momentary happenings.

THANKFULNESS

The natural man feels a genuine joy at receiving a gift, in
obtaining something he has not earned. The pious man knows
that nothing he has has been earned; not even his perceptions,
his thoughts and words, or even his life, are his deservedly.
He knows that he has no claim to anything with which he is
endowed. Knowing, therefore, that he merits little, he never
arrogates anything to himself. His thankfulness being stronger
than his wants and desires, he can live in joy and with a quiet
spirit. Being conscious of the evidences of God's blessing in

all that he receives, the natural man has two attitudes toward life—joy and gloom. The pious man has but one, for to him gloom represents an overbearing and presumptuous depreciation of underlying realities. Gloom implies that man thinks he has a right to a better, more pleasing world. Gloom is a refusal, not an offer; a snub, not an appreciation; a retreat instead of a pursuit. Gloom's roots are in pretentiousness, fastidiousness and a disregard of the good. The gloomy man, living in irritation and in a constant quarrel with his destiny, senses hostility everywhere, and seems never to be aware of the illegitimacy of his own complaints. He has a fine sense for the incongruities of life, but stubbornly refuses to recognize the delicate grace of existence.

COMMON DEEDS ARE ADVENTURES

The pious man does not take life for granted. The weighty business of living does not cloud for him the miracle of life and the consciousness that he lives through God. No routine of social or economic life dulls his mindfulness of this, the ineffably wonderful in nature and history. History to him is a perpetual improvisation by the Creator, which is being continually and violently interfered with by man; and his heart is fixed on this great mystery that is being played by God and man. Thus, his main asset is not some singular experience but life itself. Any exceptional experience serves only as a keyhole for the key of his belief. He does not depend on the exceptional, for to him commonplace deeds are adventures in the domain of the spiritual, and all his normal thoughts are, as it

288

were, sensations of the holy. He feels the hidden warmth of good in all things, and finds hints of God in almost every ordinary object on which he turns his gaze. It is for this reason that his words bring hope into a sordid and despairing world.

RESPONSIBILITY

The scope of that in which the pious man feels himself involved is not a single realm—as, for instance, that of ethical acts—but covers the whole of life. Life to him is a challenge from which he can never be free. No evasion on his part can escape it, and no sphere of action, no period of life, can be withdrawn from it. So piety cannot consist in specific acts only, such as prayer or ritual observances, but is bound up with all actions, concomitant with all doings, accompanying and shaping all life's business. Man's responsibility to God cannot be discharged by an excursion into spirituality, by making life an episode of spiritual rhapsody, the very sense of responsibility is the scaffold on which he stands as daily he goes on building life. His every deed, every incident of mind takes place on this scaffold, so that unremittingly man is at work either building up or tearing down his life, his home, his hope of God.

Responsibility implies freedom, and man who is in bondage to environment, to social ties, to inner disposition, may yet enjoy freedom before God. Only before God is man truly independent and truly free. But freedom in its turn implies responsibility, and man is responsible for the way in which he utilizes nature. It is amazing how thoughtless modern man is of his responsibility in relation to his world. He finds before him a world crammed to overflowing with wonderful materials and forces, and without hesitation or scruple he grasps at whatever is within his reach. Omnivorous in his desire, unrestrained in his efforts, tenacious in his purpose, he is gradually changing the face of the earth; and there seems to be none to deny him or challenge his eminence. Deluded by this apparent greatness, we give no thought to the question of what basis there is for our assumed right to possess our universe. Our own wayward desires and impulses, however natural they may be, are no title to ownership. Unmindful of this, we take our title for granted and grasp at everything, never questioning whether this may not be robbery. Powerhouse, factory and department store make us familiar with the exploitation of nature for our benefit. And lured by familiarity, the invisible trap for the mind, we easily yield to the illusion that these things are rightfully at our disposal, and think little of the sun, the rainfall, the water courses, as sources by no means rightfully our own. It is only when we suddenly come up against things obviously beyond the scope of human domination or jurisdiction, such as mountains or oceans, or uncontrollable events like sudden death, earthquakes, or other catastrophes, that we are somewhat shaken out of our illusions.

In reality man has not unlimited powers over the earth, as he has not over stars or winds. He has not even complete power over himself. In the absolute sense, neither the world nor his own life belongs to him. And of the things he does more or less control, he controls not the essence but only the appearance, as is evident to anyone who has ever looked with unclouded vision in the face of even a flower or a stone. The

290

question then is: Who is the lord? Who owns all that exists? "The earth is the Lord's." So the pious man regards the forces of nature, the thoughts of his own mind, life and destiny, as the property of God. Such regard governs his attitude toward all things. He does not grumble when calamities befall him, or lapse into despair; for he knows that all in life is the concern of the divine, because all that is, is in the divine possession.

A PERPETUAL GIFT

Thus the pious man realizes, also, that whatever he may have at his disposal has been bestowed upon him as a gift. And there is a difference between a possession and a gift. Possession is loneliness. The very word excludes others from the use of the possessed object without the consent of the possessor, and those who insist on possession ultimately perish in self-excommunication and loneliness. On the other hand, in receiving a gift the recipient obtains, besides the present, also the love of the giver. A gift is thus the vessel that contains the affection, which is destroyed as soon as the recipient begins to look on it as a possession. The pious man avers that he has a perpetual gift from God, for in all that comes to him he feels the love of God. In all the thousand and one experiences that make up a day, he is conscious of that love intervening in his life.

291

The ordinary man is inclined to disregard all indications of the presence of the divine in life. In his conceit and vainglory he thinks of himself as the possessor. But this is sacrilege to the pious man, and his method of saving himself from such hallucination is by asceticism and sacrifice. He rids himself of all sense of being a possessor by giving up, for God's sake, things that are desired or valued, and by depriving himself, for the sake of others who need his help, of those things that are precious to him. Thus, to sacrifice is not to abandon what has been granted to us, to throw away the gifts of life. It is, on the contrary, giving back to God what we have received from Him by employing it in His service. Such giving is a form of thanksgiving.

Both self-dispossession and offering are essential elements of sacrifice. Mere offering without self-dispossession would be without personal participation and could easily lapse into a superficial ritual act in which the mechanical aspect is more important than the personal. It would result in externalization and perfunctoriness of sacrifice, as has so often happened in the history of religion. On the other hand, self-dispossession alone tends to make asceticism an end in itself, and when turned into an end in itself it loses its bearing upon God. True asceticism is not merely depriving ourselves, but giving to God what is precious to us.

Poverty has often been an ideal for pious men, but a man may be poor in material goods while yet clinging the more tenaciously to his ambitions and intellectual goods. Mere poverty in itself is not a good, for the bitterness of poverty often upsets the balance of values in human character, while the delight of the righteous man in the gifts of God affords him strength to serve and the means to give. The purpose of sacrifice does not lie in self-pauperization as such, but in the yielding of all aspirations to God, thus creating space for Him in the heart. Moreover it is an *imitatio Dei,* for it is done after the manner of the divine Giver, and reminds man that he is created in the likeness of the divine, and is thus related to God.

KINSHIP WITH THE DIVINE

This, however, presents another problem. How are we to understand this kinship of man with the divine? One indication of man's affinity with God is his persistent aspiration to go beyond himself. He has an ability to devote himself to a higher aim, the potentiality of a will to serve, to dedicate himself to a task which goes beyond his own interests and his own life, to live for an ideal. This ideal may be the family, a friend, a group, the nation, or it may be art, science or social service. In many persons this will to serve is suppressed, but in the pious man it blooms and flourishes. In many lives these ideals seem blind alleys, but in the pious man they are thoroughfares to God. If these ideals become idols, ends in themselves, they hem the soul in, but to the pious man they are openings letting in the light from far places to illumine many an insignificant detail. To him ideals are strides on the way, never the destination.

293

Piety, finally, is allegiance to the will of God. Whether that will is understood or not, it is accepted as good and holy, and is obeyed in faith. Life is a mandate, not the enjoyment of an annuity; a task, not a game; a command, not a favor. So to the pious man life never appears as a fatal chain of events following necessarily one on another, but comes as a voice with an appeal. It is a flow of opportunity for service, every experience giving the clue to a new duty, so that all that enters life is for him a means of showing renewed devotion. Piety is, thus, not an excess of enthusiasm, but implies a resolve to follow a definite course of life in pursuit of the will of God. All the pious man's thoughts and plans revolve around this concern, and nothing can distract him or turn him from the way. Whoever sets out on this way soon learns how imperious is the spirit. He senses the compulsion to serve, and though at times he may attempt to escape, the strength of this compulsion will bring him back inevitably to the right way in search of the will of God. Before he acts, he will pause to weigh the effects of his act in the scales of God. Before he speaks, he will consider whether his words will be well pleasing to Him. Thus, in self-conquest and earnest endeavor, with sacrifice and single-mindedness, through prayer and grace, he proceeds on his way, and to him the way is more important than the goal. It is not his destiny to accomplish but to contribute, and his will to serve shapes his entire conduct. His preoccupation with the will of God is not limited to a section of his activities, but his great desire is to place his whole life at the disposal of God. In

294

this he finds the real meaning of life. He would feel wretched and lost without the certainty that his life, insignificant though it be, is of some purpose in the great plan, and life takes on enhanced value when he feels himself engaged in fulfilling purposes which lead him away from himself. In this way, he feels that in whatever he does, he is ascending step by step a ladder leading to the ultimate. In aiding a creature, he is helping the Creator. In succoring the poor, he fulfills a concern of God. In admiring the good, he reveres the spirit of God. In loving the pure, he is drawn to Him. In promoting the right, he is directing things toward His will, in which all aims must terminate. Ascending by this ladder, the pious man reaches the state of self-forgetfulness, sacrificing not only his desires but also his will; for he realizes that it is the will of God that matters, and not his own perfection or salvation. Thus, the glory of man's devotion to the good becomes a treasure of God on earth.

OUR DESTINY IS TO AID

The greatest problem is not how to continue but how to exalt our existence. The cry for a life beyond the grave is presumptuous, if there is no cry for eternal life prior to our descending to the grave. Eternity is not perpetual future but perpetual presence. He has planted in us the seed of eternal life. The world to come is not only a hereafter but also a *herenow*.

Our greatest problem is not how to continue but how to return. "How can I repay unto the Lord all his bountiful dealings with me?" (Psalms 116:12). When life is an answer, death is a home-coming. "Precious in the sight of the Lord is the death of his saints" (Psalms 116:14). For our greatest problem is but a resonance of God's concern: How can I repay unto man all his bountiful dealings with me? "For the mercy of God endureth forever."

This is the meaning of existence: To reconcile liberty with service, the passing with the lasting, to weave the threads of temporality into the fabric of eternity.

The deepest wisdom man can attain is to know that his destiny is to aid, to serve. We have to conquer in order to succumb; we have to acquire in order to give away; we have to triumph in order to be overwhelmed. Man has to understand in order to believe, to know in order to accept. The aspiration is to obtain; the perfection is to dispense. This is the meaning of death: the ultimate self-dedication to the divine. Death so understood will not be distorted by the craving for immortality, for this act of giving away is reciprocity on man's part for God's gift of life. For the pious man it is a privilege to die.

Index

Index

299

Index

Index

My thanks are due to Doctor Fritz Kaufmann of the University of Buffalo for his kindness in reading the manuscript. Chapter 26 of this book was first published in the *Review of Religion*, 1942; parts of chapters 17 and 22 in the *Journal of Religion*, 1943; and in the *Reconstructionist*, 1944. I am grateful to the editors for permission to reproduce the material.